Looking for Angels

Looking for Angels

by

Steven P. Osborne

Ark Press
Salt Lake City, Utah

Ark Press is a division of Morson Publishing
Morson Publishing
P.O. Box 21713
Salt Lake City, Utah 84121–0713

Published 1996
Printed in the United States of America

Cover designed by Reed L. Perkins

Printed by Patterson Printing, Benton Harbor, MI

ISBN 1–878423–23–1

Contents

*To the angels in my life ...
with and without tangible bodies.*

Foreword

I drove a taxi at night during my last few years of college. Even on the relatively tame streets of Salt Lake City in the mid 1970s, I became all too familiar with the faces of those who have been given many names by many writers: the lost ones, *les misérables,* the damned. I have never been able to break the haunting spell those faces cast over my soul. Their expressions—which ranged from empty to terrified, from lonely to defeated—remain in my memory like a kaleidoscope of human suffering.

I wrote this book for them—for all of us because we are all them.

At times we all feel alone and unloved. At times we all look for meaning in our lives and see nothing. At times we all search desperately for eternity beyond mortality, and find only the blackness of death.

But the moment we see an angel, or genuinely believe a story about one, those feelings disappear just as darkness vanishes when a bright light is turned on. Angels tell us—with a certainty that even near-death experiences cannot—that dying is not the end of us, but merely a change of venue. When we open our hearts to the reality of angels, we come face to face with the exciting, exalting realization that there is something within us that trembles with immortality.

That is not all we learn from angels. The moment we understand at the heart level that benevolent, otherworldly beings watch over us, we are forced to accept the life-changing reality that we are never really alone, that our lives have meaning, and (most importantly) that we are loved.

It has been over 20 years since I drove a taxi. But I continue to see the despairing faces of the lost ones almost everywhere I go. I want to grab these people by the shoulders and tell them everything I know and everything I believe about angels. I know it would help, if they only believed. But I am too reserved for that, and they would probably think me crazy.

So I wrote this book. If it chases away a little darkness in a world that desperately needs light, it will have been worth the trouble.

And now a few technical notes ...

With only one exception, all the contemporary stories that are found in this book were shared with me by individuals whom I know personally. Most I know quite well. The exception happens to be the friend of one of my friends. All these people are sane, "normal" people, and not given to flights of fancy. In gathering the angel stories for this book, I resisted the temptation to grab stories wherever I could find them. (Some writers have even advertised for angel stories, which I feel opens the door to stories that spring from questionable motives). I decided early on that I would use only those personal experiences that came directly to me from the people around me—individuals whom I could personally interview, so that I could feel the truth and sincerity in what they were saying ... or the lack of it.

At first I worried that I had limited myself to the point that I wouldn't be able to find enough angel stories to fill a comic book. I was wrong. Personal accounts involving heavenly beings began to pour out of the hearts of friends, family members, and neighbors.

This overwhelming experience told me that encounters with angels are much more common than I had ever suspected.

Of course, there is no way to prove to your rational mind that the stories about angels you will read in this book actually took place. Your own heart must tell you that. If it does, no further proof is needed. I should mention that I didn't use all the stories I heard. I had asked for the gift of discernment in this project, and that gift told me not to use a few of the accounts that came my way. Every one of the stories that did end up in this book felt "right" to me. I hope they will feel right to you.

Also, rather than merely recount one angel story after another, I have tried to present these experiences in a theological context, doing my best to answer common questions that arise and using the accounts of angelic encounters as illustrations.

I should point out that I did not use in this book the real names of the people who were kind enough to share their sacred stories with me. It wasn't their idea to keep their identities confidential. It was mine. I simply wanted to safeguard their privacy—especially in matters of such a spiritually sensitive nature.

As you read this book, it would be impossible not to notice my frequent use of Mormon scriptures and historical works, and references to the writings of noted Mormon prophets and theologians, both living and dead. Although I am a practicing Mormon, it was not by default that I used my own church's literature so extensively. In my search for angels, I ranged freely through the pages of the Muslim *Koran*, the Hindu *Bhagavad Gita*, "new age" literature, as well as Buddhist, Taoist, and Confucian texts. But, like the fortune hunter who traveled the world over in search of a treasure, only to return exhausted and discover that it had been in his own back yard all along, I discovered that the richest source of angel theology and experiences was to be found in my own theological backyard. For this reason, this book approaches the subject of angels primarily from the theological and experiential base rock of Mormonism. It is a solid foundation.

However, this is not a book about Mormonism. It is a book about angels, and angels transcend all religious organizations. It is written for people of all faiths—even for those who claim they have no faith. Regardless of where you fall theologically, I hope that reading it will nudge you a little closer to God, however you define God.

One final note: I do not think that the forces of darkness wanted me to finish this book. I say this because my life has been an emotional roller coaster ever since I started it. The closer I came to finishing it, the more difficult it was to go on. One thing after another came along to tie up my time and keep me busy with other things. Worse, from an emotional standpoint, it became almost physically painful to do the final writing.

On a beautiful Saturday in the early summer, I finally gritted my teeth and dug in, determined to bring it to an end. As I wrote, the oppressive feeling about the book that had been weighing down on me lifted for no apparent reason, and I was engulfed by a feeling of holiness. Sitting there in my office, I felt as if I was in a temple. There have been only a few times in my life when the veil between this world and the spiritual realm has become tissue-thin. That was one of them.

In that spiritual cocoon, I finished the book.

Steve Osborne
Salt Lake City
July 15, 1995

Chapter 1
The Quest Begins

*"There are more things in heaven and earth, Horatio,
than are dreamt of in your philosophy."*
— *William Shakespeare*, Hamlet

A few years ago a friend of mine named Paul told me a story that both inspired and disturbed me ...

It happened in the late 1970s, during an L.D.S. sacrament meeting. Although Paul had been raised in a very active Mormon family, he had fallen away from the church years before. He was only there that day to support his family. His infant niece was to be blessed.

During the meeting, Paul, who had been sitting next to his wife, suddenly left his body and found himself looking down on the congregation from above. He said he felt a spiritual presence at his right side—a personage who looked like a bright flame. But he didn't see this being distinctly. "There was something between us." he recalled, "I can't describe it. It was like a veil made of all sorts of layers of gauze. He was on the outside, and I was on the inside."

The angel spoke without speaking. Paul felt as if the words were coming from deep within his spiritual core. "Look!" the angel commanded, pointing down at the congregation. Paul looked and saw the people sitting in the pews, as before. He had known many of these people since childhood. Friends, family members, and old acquaintances were gathered there for the blessing.

But now he saw something more—something startling and beautiful: brilliant bands of white connected the married couples below him, many of which he knew to have been married in Mormon temples. These were not fuzzy, hazy bands of energy. They were distinct and solid-looking, and ran like arches from the heart of one spouse to the heart of the other.

Paul remembers a feeling of motion, a sensation that he can only describe as moving through a sort of tunnel with the radiant presence at his side. "You will have this [kind of marriage]," said the angel, and then added, "The gospel is true." Then, as quickly as it began, he found himself back in his body sitting next to his wife. "Did you see that?" he asked her. She hadn't.

Dazzled and bewildered by the strange event, Paul—who hadn't even believed in angels until then—struggled to understand its meaning. Why did it happen to him? And why then? But answers didn't come. Then, just two days later, he discovered that his wife had been unfaithful to him for some time, with more than one man. Their marriage had not been good. Paul was well aware of that. Nevertheless, the discovery was shattering.

"I'd never had much luck with relationships even before my marriage," Paul said. "And there I was facing the reality of a failed marriage. I really think that if I hadn't seen what I saw during that meeting—those bands of white uniting the hearts of married couples—I don't think I would have ever tried again after our divorce."

But he did try again, thanks to the message he received that pivotal Sunday at the side of an angel. He met a beautiful, talented woman, and they are now happily married with two wonderful children.

That was not the end of Paul's story, however. His experience with the angel launched him on a spiritual quest. He began to go to church again, and plunged into an intense study of Mormon theology, reading everything he could get his hands on, including many out-of-print and hard-to-find texts. He did not limit his search to the L.D.S. theological arena, however. He began pondering some of the world's most esoteric spiritual texts from both the Eastern and Western worlds. Every religion, every mystical school of thought were fair game to him. He immersed himself in them.

This went on for ten years. Then came a crisis. "I felt like I had followed the spirit," Paul told me. "But I came to the point where my consciousness started to shift, and I got really scared because I started seeing things differently. I was going through a spiritual crisis of following the spirit and fearing greatly where it was leading me. It was so different than anything that I could conceive of.

"I knew that I had come to the point where I was going to have to literally let go of so many things that my life had been built on: temporal kinds of supports, the world view I had inherited from my parents and our culture, even a lot of things I'd been taught in church. I was finding that there was so much more. I was realizing that there were deeper ramifications and meanings to things than we are taught in church—meanings that most people just pay lip service to. I was starting to feel that these things were much more real and profound than I had ever conceived them to be. And it was frightening me.

"What I had learned was not leading me *away* from the church. It was taking me *deeper*. It was a very spiritual time, but very, very scary. It was a time of having to go on pure faith. But I knew I couldn't take it much longer. I literally thought I was going crazy. So I began to pray with my whole heart.

"I said, 'Look, I feel like I've followed you. I've followed every bit of the spirit, and yet I feel very scared. I feel like I might be going in the wrong direction. I don't know what's going on. I'm afraid. I wish you were with me.'"

At that moment, Paul felt a distinct presence at his right side, just as he had at that sacrament meeting over a decade before. And he heard the voice, in the same way he heard it before.

It said, *"I've never left you."*

Turning to the presence, Paul's attention was drawn down toward the floor by an intensely bright light. "It looked like a veil was being lifted from the ground up," he explained. "As it was raised, I saw two feet, and then the bottom of what looked like a robe. Everything was brilliantly white. Then the veil started lifting higher, and I couldn't handle it. I freaked out. And the instant I did, the veil dropped and I saw no more.

"I wish I hadn't been so afraid," said Paul, thinking back. "But at the time it was very startling. It was so real—more real than anything I had experienced in my life."

<hr>

Paul's story went straight to my core. Something told me it was true—every word of it. And because it was true, it inspired me. But for the same reason, it disturbed me. Although my theological belief system forced me to accept the reality of angels on a theoretical level, it was somehow disturbing to think that they could come down and touch our lives on a very real, practical level.

I was forced to admit that I had never given angels much thought. And yet, as I looked back on my life, it occurred to me that I had had several brushes with these beings. For example, one night over a decade ago, I was forcibly evicted from my bed by a toddler who loved to snuggle down in between Tina and me as we slept. Once settled, she would alternately prod us with her knees until one of us threw in the towel and agreed to trade her beds for the night. I gave in first.

I have always been a good sleeper. I rarely wake up in the middle of the night. But several hours after I had dozed off again in my daughter's room, I awoke for no apparent reason and saw something that I will never forget. There, standing around the edge of the bed and looking down at me in silence were the dark silhouettes of several men. At first I thought I was dreaming, but it soon became clear that I wasn't. I could move, feel myself, and see other objects in the room as clearly as the moonlight coming in through the window allowed. I was definitely awake.

The visitors stood like sentinels. They didn't move or speak, and didn't seem to care that I was staring back at them. I couldn't see their faces, only their dark silhouettes, which showed just a hint of dimension. When I reached out to touch the presence that was closest to me, they all disappeared.

Since that night I have had a half dozen similar experiences involving one or more of these night sentinels. I have wondered if they were demons or guardian angels; whether they were there to protect me from some danger, charge me up, or communicate an important message directly to my heart.

How many other times in my life I have been the beneficiary of angelic intervention I can't begin to guess. I'm sure I don't give my guardian angels a fraction of the credit they deserve.

There was, for example, a night in Panama City when I was killing time walking around downtown. I wandered past a theater and decided to go in and watch a movie. I had nothing better to do. But for some reason I felt impressed to turn away at the last moment, and continued walking down the street. An hour later, I was returning to my hotel and passed by the theater again. But something had happened: the street in front of it was choked with fire trucks, police cars, and rescue vehicles, their lights flashing. Rescue workers were frantically digging through the rubble that had once been the movie theater. The roof had caved in, burying everyone who had been watching the movie I had inexplicably decided not to see.

Did an angel whisper into my ear that night, telling me to keep walking? I don't know. But the more I learn about these guiding presences, the more I suspect that they play a far more pivotal role in our lives than we would imagine.

After I heard Paul's story, and began to reflect on certain occurrences in my own life (some of which I will recount later), I knew that angels would never again be a non-issue for me. I am one of those people who are blessed, or perhaps cursed, with a driving curiosity about spiritual things. I knew I had to find out who these otherworldly entities are, why they help us, and how. I knew I had to break through to the other side and see what was there.

And so the journey began.

Chapter 2
A Dead End Along the Path—
Defining the Elephant's Tail

Time may come when Men
With Angels may participate ...
Meanwhile enjoy,
Your fill, what happiness this happy state
Can comprehend, incapable of more.
          — *John Milton,* Paradise Lost

My search for angels and the truth about them got off to a rocky start: I decided to become a scholar.

After all, didn't I have over 4,000 of the world's greatest unabridged literary and religious works sitting on my desk on a few CD-ROM discs? Didn't I have the electronic capability to search through them with lightning speed for all references to angels, guardians, spirits, and other related words and phrases? And didn't I also have on my desk two CD-ROMs packed with all the scriptures of my own church, plus hundreds of other volumes written by Mormon leaders and scholars throughout the church's history?

Yes, scholarship was only a few clicks of the mouse away. I would dive in and quickly get my hands on the true, undisputed, universal definition of the nature of angels. I would become an authority on the subject, backed by hard, straight facts. I would become infallibly knowledgeable. Then I could get back to thinking about fly fishing.

Several weeks later, with reams of angel references stacked on my desk from almost every culture and religion in the world, I closed my bloodshot eyes, buried my face in my hands, and vowed to lose myself in some corner of the earth where I would never hear the word "angel" again.

My problem? There were no straight answers—no uncontested definitions. No one seemed to agree on who angels are, where they come from, what they look like, how they work, and why God needs them in the first place. (Why would he need them if he's all-powerful?) I was killing myself trying to find needles of consensus in haystacks of opinions. Through some cosmic foul-up, God had failed to set angels in concrete so as not to confuse mankind.

Even my own church failed me. While it proved to be the most fertile source of information and experiences about angels I found, it didn't authoritatively answer my questions. The Prophet Joseph Smith, the founder of the Mormon Church, said that angels were resurrected beings, as opposed to "ministering spirits," which were people that had died but were not yet resurrected. But Mormon apostles Parley P. Pratt, John Widtsoe, and others said angels could also be spirits that hadn't been resurrected yet, or perhaps hadn't even come to earth yet. Joseph Smith received a revelation which said that every angel who ministers here on this earth belongs to or has belonged to this earth. And yet in another revelation he talks about translated personages who become "ministering angels unto many planets." Some writings by church authorities indicate that we all have guardian angels all the time. Others say that they come to us only when they have a job to do. These apparent conflicts and ambiguities were just the tip of the iceberg.

Why in heaven's name didn't my church do what any self-respecting organized religion would do and nail it down with hard, sure doctrine? Why didn't the church fathers just say, "This

is the way it is; end of discussion," and then throw out everybody
who disagreed?

Just at the point that I was wishing I owned a dog so I could
kick it across the floor, I remembered the story of the blind men
and the elephant. It goes like this:

THE BLIND MEN AND THE ELEPHANT

It was six men of Indostan
To learning much inclined,
Who went to see the elephant
(Though all of them were blind),
That each by observation
Might satisfy his mind.

The First approached the elephant,
And, happening to fall
Against his broad and sturdy side,
At once began to bawl:
"God bless me! but the elephant
Is nothing but a wall!"

The Second, feeling of the tusk,
Cried: "Ho! what have we here
So very round and smooth and sharp?
To me 'tis mighty clear
This wonder of an elephant
Is very like a spear!"

The Third approached the animal,
And, happening to take
The squirming trunk within his hands,
Thus boldly up and spake:
"I see," quoth he, "the elephant
Is very like a snake."

The Fourth reached out his eager hand,
And felt about the knee:
"What most this wondrous beast is like
Is mighty plain," quoth he;
"'Tis clear enough the elephant
Is very like a tree."

The Fifth, who chanced to touch the ear,
Said: "E'en the blindest man
Can tell what this resembles most;
Deny the fact who can,
This marvel of an elephant
Is very like a fan!"

The Sixth no sooner had begun
About the beast to grope,
Than, seizing on the swinging tail
That fell within his scope,
"I see," quoth he, "the elephant
Is very like a rope!"

And so these men of Indostan
Disputed loud and long,
Each in his own opinion
Exceeding stiff and strong,
Though each was partly in the right,
And all were in the wrong!

So, oft in theologic wars
The disputants, I ween,
Rail on in utter ignorance
Of what each other mean,
And prate about an elephant

The message of this wonderful story set me free.

In my left-brained quest for "the definitive angel," I had forgotten that when it comes to spiritual matters—whether we're trying to define the nature of God or of angels—we're like blind men touching only one part of an elephant's anatomy. We each come away with a different piece of the puzzle. The Apostle Paul was right: "we see through a glass, darkly," and "we know in part." In our attempt to define the complete elephant, I touch the tail and the beast is a rope, while you touch its leg and it is a tree. We are both a little right, but a lot wrong. The true essence of the elephant eludes us.

* * *

"But there has been a great difficulty in getting anything into the heads of this generation. It has been like splitting hemlock knots with a corn-dodger for a wedge, and a pumpkin for a beetle. Even the Saints are slow to understand.

I have tried for a number of years to get the minds of the Saints prepared to receive the things of God; but we frequently see some of them, after suffering all they have for the work of God, will fly to pieces like glass as soon as anything comes that is contrary to their traditions: they cannot stand the fire at all."
— *Joseph Smith*

It hit me with force that we have no business trying to pin down and dissect angels. Instead, we should gratefully accept the conflicting perspectives and opinions about them and look for hints within them that could give us a wider glimpse of the full picture. Our tight definitions, which are so often dictated by our cultural and intellectual traditions, limit our vision.

Besides, definitions are not what religion is all about. One of my favorite statements is by a great teacher from India named Paramhansa Yogananda. He said, "How would you explain the taste of an orange to someone who had never tasted one? You could never do so adequately. The goal of religion is not to define God accurately. It is to inspire in people the desire to commune with Him—to experience Him in inner silence, in their souls ... No master is concerned with formulating absolute definitions. What he hopes, simply, is to convey a suggestion of the divine experience."

What Yogananda says about defining God is equally true of defining angels. Our attempts to rigidly say "angels are this, and they are not that" will only bring them down to our level, when what we need is to be lifted up to theirs. It's like the poet, John Keats, said: "Philosophy will clip an angel's wings." Their full essence can never be captured in words. Yet words can inspire us to open our minds and our spiritual eyes and ears to the angels that surround us, and to experience them joyously in our lives.

"Could we read and comprehend all that has been written from the days of Adam, on the relation of man to God and angels in a future state, we should know very little about it," said Joseph Smith. "Could you gaze into heaven five minutes, you would know more than you would by reading all that ever was written on the subject."

That's our goal: to get a glimpse of heaven. And this is our challenge: to find the golden strands of truth that run through the differing experiences and insights we read about angels; to rejoice in the spirit of the words, rather than sulk in the conflicting details. Once we leave the level plain of skepticism and begin looking for footholds of belief on the steep path of faith, angels will lift us higher than we ever could climb on our own, and visions of truth and glory will open to us that would otherwise remain closed.

Chapter 3
In the Household of Faith

"In this situation we frequently hold communion with our departed father, mother, brother, sister, son or daughter, or with the former husband or wife of our bosom whose affections for us, being rooted and grounded in the eternal elements, issuing from under the sanctuary of love's eternal fountain, can never be lessened or diminished by death, distance of space, or length of years."
— *Parley P. Pratt*

Having traveled the dead-end street of scholarship, I passed through the gates of faith and started out once more on my quest to know angels. Guided by faith rather than facts, doors began to open. Every time I turned around, I bumped into people with angel stories that opened the doors of my understanding a little wider and touched my heart a little deeper.

Case in point: I was talking to some friends after a class I was taking one night, and someone asked if I was involved in any interesting writing projects. I said I'd been thinking a lot about angels, and was probably going to write a book on the subject. One of the people there that night—Katherine, the sister-in-law of a family friend—had recently been divorced, and had suffered the agonizing loss of a 15-month-old child just a month before.

Just before the next class, Katherine sat down beside me. There was a sense of peace and hope about her that I hadn't felt the week before. She asked if I was still going to write a book about angels. When I said I was, she said she had something she wanted to tell me. After the class, she related the following experience, which she later was kind enough to write down:

My daughter, Olivia, died when she was 15 months old after a long hospitalization. She was born with birth defects and in spite of many pioneering surgeries, she was unable to breathe properly. Olivia looked like a cherub. She had blond hair, large blue eyes, a robust body, and more courage than most adults.

It was less than a month after she had passed away, and I was grieving terribly. I could not understand why an innocent baby had been born with fatal birth defects that caused her agonizing pain, and why my child, whom I adored, could be taken away from me. Although my mother, who was very close to Olivia, had seen her in a dream, I had yet to experience the privilege of a visit and was a little jealous.

My parents invited me, along with my brother and his wife, to a live performance at Abravenel Hall featuring the art of James C. Christensen and the music of Kurt Bestor, Evening Angels. *I was reluctant to go at first, but then capitulated. The music was sublime, with melodic harps and flutes as one might imagine angels playing. As the full orchestra began to play, I relaxed and was soon transported to a divine realm. It was then that I realized that Olivia was sitting in my lap. I shifted my weight to accommodate her little body, brushed a golden strand of hair from her forehead, and looked at her as she gazed up into my face. She smiled, then crinkled her nose and snorted as she used to do when we played.*

I was lost in joy and oblivious to whether my brother and his wife noticed my strange movements or the very tangible baby kicking her legs in my lap. Olivia seemed content to play with me, and we sat snuggling and holding each other throughout the rest of the concert.

The presentation came to an end all too soon, and the hall exploded with applause as the audience gave the two talented men a standing ovation. As I looked over the crowd, to my amazement, I saw hordes of angels. Almost every person there was accompanied by an angel. The rustling of their large, feathered wings was an audible sound. Then, for a instant, my rational mind doubted what I saw and Olivia disappeared. But I was left with a profound feeling of a divine order, and the peaceful assurance that Olivia was happy.

— Katherine

Angel experiences are often family affairs. "What a pleasing thought," wrote the early Mormon apostle Parley P. Pratt, "that many who minister to us, and watch over us, are our near kindred, our fathers who have died and risen again in former ages, and who watch over their descendants with all the parental care and solicitude which characterize affectionate fathers and mothers on the earth."

Joseph F. Smith, the sixth President of the L.D.S. Church, elaborated on this idea: "... when messengers are sent to minister to the inhabitants of this earth," he said, "they are not strangers, but from the ranks of our kindred friends, and fellow-beings and fellow-servants ... Our fathers and mothers, brothers, sisters and friends who have passed away from this earth, having been faithful, and worthy to enjoy these rights and privileges, may have a mission given them to visit their friends and relatives upon the earth again, bringing from the divine presence messages of love, of warning, of reproof or instruction, to those whom they had learned to love in the flesh."

Although neither of these men specifically refer to departed children ministering to their living parents, Katherine's experience tells us that this does in fact happen, and adds another loving facet to the scope of angelic possibilities.

Her experience was also notable because she saw what she described as large "wings" on the angels. Yet Joseph Smith and others have said that angels don't have wings. Certainly, it doesn't seem logical that they would. Was Katherine's perception of wings on the angels colored by her previous understanding of them? Or was she actually seeing auras of light radiating around these heavenly beings—energy fields that defy exact technical description? (Squint at a candle's flame in a dark room and you will see "wings" sprout from it.) To someone overwhelmed by the glory of the experience and not paying careful attention to details—who would?—couldn't these auras be perceived as "large, feathered wings"?

Hush! my dear, lie still and slumber,
Holy angels guard thy bed!
Heavenly blessings without number
Gently falling on thy head.
— *Isaac Watts,* A Cradle Hymn

Accouterments aside, the idea of departed family members serving as angels to those who remain in the flesh is one that feels good to both the mind and the heart.

My own son, Greg, had an experience of this nature. Greg is a boy's boy. By that I mean he has always loved balls, swords, guns, and cigarette lighters, and has absolutely no aversion to dirt. Curiously, there is another side to him—a sensitive, spiritual side. Even before he could put a grammatically correct sentence together, he would occasionally surprise us by asking deep, almost mystical questions that belied a spiritual maturity few adults could claim. The same day that he would leave for school blissfully unaware that he had left his lunch, homework, shoes and socks behind, he would startle us by asking, with heart-rending anxiety, why God made poison ivy.

One night when Greg was about seven years old, I went into his bedroom for a goodnight hug. The room was dimly lit by the light that came in through the door from the hall. He had already fallen asleep, so I leaned over and kissed him on the cheek. As I turned to leave, he awoke and mumbled, "Hi Dad and Jenny."

Jenny is his older sister. But she was asleep in the next bedroom at the time. "I'm the only one here, Bud," I explained.

"But who's your friend?" he asked.

"No one else is here," I assured him. "Go back to sleep now. Sorry I woke you up." I tucked him in, brushed his hair back off his forehead, and watched as his eyes drooped and closed once again.

It wasn't until recently that Greg told me why he thought someone else was in his room that night. We had been talking about this book, and he started asking some pointed questions about who angels are and what they do. Then he told me that he was pretty sure he had seen one that night.

He explained that when he woke up, he saw me standing above him beside his bed, my profile silhouetted in the light from the hall. But there was another figure—a human form that was standing at a point beside me and then "sort of floated" down to the foot of the bed.

During the brief and confusing exchange that had followed that night, Greg said that the figure stood there innocuously at the foot of the bed doing "something weird" with his hands, as if he were fluffing up the covers around his feet. "I couldn't tell who it was," Greg recalled, "because it was just kind of like a shape that was darker than the room around it."

But when Greg asked who my friend was, the figure leaned slightly forward and brought a finger up to his lips, directing him to say no more. In leaning toward him, explained Greg, the figure's face and hand came forward out of the dark into a plane of light, as if the darkness were a vertical pool of black water from which he emerged, illuminated, to be seen.

Greg remembers the expression on the face. It was tender and pleasant, though not smiling. He saw it for only a few seconds, obeyed its signed directive to be silent, and then watched as it faded away.

Did he recognize who it was? "I didn't know who it was then," he informed me, "but I think I do now. It looked like Grandpa Shipley in that picture when he was young."

Grandpa Shipley is my wife's father. He passed away a dozen years before Greg was born. The few pictures of him that Greg had seen before that night had been taken when Shipley was older. Because of health problems later in life, he looked much different than the robust young man he had been in his 20s.

A few years after Greg saw this strange presence, Tina was given a large portrait photo of her father when he was in his early 20s. She hung it on the wall in our basement family room. When Greg saw it he made the connection. It was then that he realized it was his Grandpa Shipley who had come to tuck him into bed that night.

"I believe we are free, within limits, and yet there is an unseen hand, a guiding angel, that somehow, like a submerged propeller, drives us on." — *Rabindranath Tagore*

I have known Rachael and her family for years. Her husband died when she was in her mid-30s, leaving her with children between the ages of six and twelve to raise alone. After the early stages of grief, Rachael slipped into an extended period of anger and bitterness. In addition to having to cope with her own devastated emotions, she was having serious problems with her children. She cursed her departed husband for not being there to help. She hated him for abandoning her—for leaving her to handle all the problems she was facing by herself.

In the midst of her traumas, something happened that made her realize that she was *not* alone. It happened early one morning, before sunrise. She awoke abruptly, lying on her back in bed. There was a weight on top of her, as if someone were stretched out on top of her body. Yet she was alone. She tried to move, but couldn't. The weight was too heavy. Something very real but completely invisible was pinning her to the bed.

The expected reaction would be to struggle, to panic. Yet she didn't. Instead, she willingly surrendered to an intimate warmth that she hadn't felt for a long time. She lay there for several minutes, the weight paralyzing yet welcome. She saw nothing; heard nothing, smelled nothing; yet knew with a certainty beyond reason that this weight was her husband. He had come back to her—if only for a few precious minutes—to try to give her strength and comfort the only way he knew how.

In the difficult few years that followed, Rachael's husband visited her on several other occasions, always in the same way, and always when she was desperately in need of strength.

I knew another woman who had a series of similar experiences. Like Rachael, she felt a paralyzing weight on her as she lay on her back in bed, yet neither heard nor saw anything else. This happened on several different occasions during a period of time when she was dealing with some painful emotional issues. Like Rachael, she too knew that it was her departed husband, trying to give her strength from the other side.

... for whoso disbelieves in God, and His angels, and His
Apostle, and the last day, has erred a wide error. —Koran

Angelic ministrations from departed family members can even include babysitting assignments.

A close friend of ours, Bonnie, read a story to me that her grandmother, Phoebe, dictated to her mother two months before her 80th birthday. Phoebe grew up in Cardston, Alberta, Canada. Her mother was a midwife. One night, she was called out to deliver a baby. Her husband went along to help take care of the woman's other children during the delivery, even though some of their own children were sick in bed.

While they were gone, Phoebe's sister, Ann, woke up delirious. She grabbed the burning-hot "fancy piece" off the stove with her bare hand and ran around hitting the children with it who were sick in bed. She didn't know what she was doing. She didn't even realize that her hand was burning. Phoebe's oldest brother, Sam, whispered "Let's pray." They knelt down and asked the Lord to bless Ann that she'd get back in bed.

It was just after the prayer that a man came into the house. The older children recognized him as their departed grandfather—their mother's father. When he entered, Ann felt the burning in her hand and dropped the stove piece. He walked over to Ann's bed and she, in turn, went to her bed and got in, no longer delirious.

"Father and mother came home as soon as they could after the baby was born," said Phoebe, "but it was several hours later. Father helped mother out of the wagon and went out to the barn to put the horses away. When mother walked into the room, Grandfather glided out. He was dressed in his temple robes, like those he was buried in. Mae and Sam told Mother of Grandfather's coming, and showed her Grandfather's picture on the wall, declared that it was he who had come and taken care of them.

"That has always been a testimony to the family of the Lord's goodness to us," she concluded.

So many angel stories turn out to be family affairs that you have to wonder if family ties don't exist even when such connections aren't readily apparent. Ultimately, of course, we're *all* family, and heavenly relationships are very likely more extensive and intimate than our earth-bound vision discloses.

"The family," said historians Will and Ariel Durant, "is the nucleus of civilization." Judging from the stories we hear about angels, the family is also the nucleus of heaven.

Chapter 4
To Serve and Protect

"Also, I saw Elder Brigham Young standing in a strange land, in the far south and west, in a desert place, upon a rock in the midst of about a dozen men of color, who appeared hostile. He was preaching to them in their own tongue, and the angel of God standing above his head, with a drawn sword in his hand, protecting him, but he did not see it."
— *Joseph Smith*

Angels have many different types of assignments—pleasant and unpleasant—but what they do most is help. "The main service of angels on earth is clearly to be helpers to humankind," said Mormon apostle and scholar, John A. Widtsoe. "They are watchmen, protecting and ministering to us in hours of need."

Listen to what some of the leaders of the L.D.S. church have said about what angels do for us:

Brigham Young: *"Teach the children to pray, that when they are large enough to go into the field with their father, they may have faith that if they are in danger they will be protected. Teach them that those good angels that are ministering spirits, and their angels, to guard and defend the just and pure, watch over them continually."*

Heber C. Kimball: *"... angels are our associates, they are with us and round about us, and watch over us, and take care of us, and lead us, and guide us, and administer to our wants in their ministry and in their holy calling unto which they are appointed."*

Heber J. Grant (in a message from the First Presidency): *"The Lord loves you. His angels are always near to help you. Your guardian angels stand by to see that no harm shall touch you, no evil thought disturb you."*

John A. Widtsoe: *"Undoubtedly angels often guard us from accidents and harm, from temptation and sin. They may properly be spoken of as guardian angels. Many people have borne and may bear testimony to the guidance and protection that they have received from sources beyond their natural vision."*

In my search for angels, I have discovered that a belief in guardian angels is widespread throughout the human race, regardless of faith or culture. In the *Story of Buddha*, we read, "From the time the Future Buddha was thus conceived, four angels with swords in their hands kept guard, to ward off all harm from both the Future Buddha and the Future Buddha's mother." The Koran says that God "sends to them guardian angels ..." Even fairy tales speak of guardian angels, as we read in the following example from the Brothers Grimm's *Snow-White and Rose-Red*:

> *Once when they had spent the night in the wood and the dawn had roused them, they saw a beautiful child in a shining white dress sitting near their bed. He got up and looked quite kindly at them, but said nothing and went away into the forest. And when they looked round they found that they had been sleeping quite close to a precipice, and would certainly have fallen into it in the darkness if they had gone only a few paces further. And their mother told them that it must have been the angel who watches over good children.*

Satan himself admitted to the divine calling of guardian angels. When he was tempting Jesus after his 40-day fast, he said, "For it is written, He shall give his angels charge over thee, to keep thee: And in [their] hands they shall bear thee up, lest at any time thou dash thy foot against a stone." (Luke, 4:10, 11.)

Clearly, a belief in guardian angels is more than a passing spiritual fad for religious weirdos and new age freaks. It is a belief that was around long before the birth of today's major religions, is an accepted theological concept today, and will likely survive and prosper in whatever spiritual environment awaits us in the future.

Do we *all* have guardian angels? Obviously, Christ did. But what about the rest of us? Are protective beings assigned to keep *us* and bear *us* up, as well? Brigham Young, the second president of the L.D.S. church, said yes. "All people have their guardian angels," he stated, "Whether our departed dead guard us is not for me to say. I can say we have our guardian angels."

Okay. We all have our personal guardian angels. At least one. But that begs another question: are they with us *all* the time? In *Evidences and* Reconciliations, Widtsoe wrote:

> *The common belief, however, that to every person born into the world is assigned a guardian angel to be with that person constantly, is not supported by available evidence. It is a very comforting thought, but at present without proof of its correctness. An angel may be a guardian angel though he come only as assigned to give us special help. In fact, the constant presence of the Holy Ghost would seem to make such a constant, angelic companionship unnecessary.*
>
> *So, until further knowledge is obtained, we may say that angels may be sent to guard us according to our need; but we cannot say with certainty that there is a special guardian angel, to be with every person constantly.*

I like Widtsoe. Unlike many of the world's philosophers and theologians, he didn't succumb to the temptation of elevating speculation and opinion to the level of cast-in-granite gospel. He merely said that current evidence didn't support the idea of *constant* angelic companionship. On the other hand, he didn't say it was out of the question. He left it wide open.

Parley P. Pratt, however, indicated that angels *are* constant companions—at least to the spiritual elite. In *Key to the Science of Theology,* he said that angels have "attended upon the footsteps of Apostles, Prophets and holy Martyrs, from the cradle to the grave." Brigham Young's directive to teach children that good angels "guard and defend the just and pure watch over them continually" also gives a sense of constant vigilance.

Frankly, I'm not nearly as anxious to know whether an angel is hovering over me 24 hours a day, seven days a week, as I am to know whether one is going to be there for me when I need him, or her. Of this there is little doubt, either from a theological or an intuitive point of view.

If individuals have guardian angels, then could we go one step further and assume that groups of people or even nations have them? Here, too, we have some assenting nods. Orson Hyde, a Mormon apostle and contemporary of Joseph Smith, referred more than once to "the guardian angel of these United States," and "the guardian angel of America."

This was not a new idea, however. Back in the 1600s, Sir Thomas Browne wrote, "Therefore for Spirits, I am so far from denying their existence, that I could easily believe, that not only whole Countries, but particular persons, have their Tutelary and Guardian Angels. It is not a new opinion of the Church of Rome, but an old one of Pythagoras and Plato; there is no heresie in it; and if not manifestly defin'd in Scripture, yet is it an opinion of a good and wholesome use in the course and actions of a man's life, and would serve as an Hypothesis to salve many doubts, whereof common Philosophy affordeth no solution."

Stories about guardian angels are not uncommon. They are just untold. Many of those who have had these experiences won't share them except with the right people and at the right time. Either they hold them too sacred to want to "cast their pearls before the swine," or they're afraid people will think they're crazy. Fortunately, when approached with sincerity by someone they trust, many will share their stories.

Behold, I send an Angel before thee,
to keep thee in the way ... — Exodus 23:20

A neighbor of mine, Andrew, is one of these people. When he heard I was writing a book about angels, he began asking me questions about it. After a discussion, during which I sensed that he wanted to tell me something, I asked him if he had had any personal encounters with angels. He seemed almost relieved when I asked, and said that he had, and that he would like to tell me about it. Here's his story:

It happened when we were first married and living in Austin, Texas. Mariam was expecting our first child, Michael, who is now 19 years old. I was finishing my master's degree in music. At that time in my life, I was in a particularly confused state of mind. I was trying to make sense of being newly married, contemplating the birth of our first child, and trying to figure out what direction my life was going to take and where all this was leading me.

I was excited for the birth of the baby, but I had so many conflicting emotions that I couldn't get into the total significance of the event. That worried me. I kept thinking that I should have been really ecstatic and excited. But I wasn't, and that was weighing down on my mind. When Mariam finally went into labor, and I still wasn't feeling as excited as I thought I should be, it bothered me even more. After all, it was the birth of our first child.

I took her to the hospital. She has babies very quickly, and they took her right into the labor room. This was just after they started allowing fathers to go into the delivery room, so they told me I could come in, but that I had to hurry. I remember changing my clothes and slipping on the gown and putting the slippers over my feet ... and still having a dark, worried feeling around me.

As they were rushing me into the delivery room, I saw, standing as if he were posted as a sentinel or a guard, a male angel with a sword, dressed in a helmet and shiny armor. There was a brilliant, white aura around him.

It happened so quickly that I couldn't really think about what I had seen, or even try to explain it to myself. It was a flash, and then I was past him and in the room where our baby was being born. But I remember distinctly that as soon as I passed the angel and walked through the door and into the delivery room, all the feelings that I had wanted to have came flooding in.

I didn't know then exactly what to think about the angel that I saw. I didn't know who it was, or what it was, or what significance it had. But since then I've read other accounts of people who have seen angels, or sentinels, or warrior angels - beings who have been there to protect them and to help them during important events in their lives.

Now I believe in my own heart that it was a warrior-type angel, or whatever you want to call it, and that it was there to protect us and make sure everything turned out all right. I think it was also there to ward off evil spirits. I was probably being followed by evil spirits. Maybe that's why I hadn't been able to experience the joy that I should have been feeling, and why I had been in such a dark state of mind.

It was as if the angel was a guard posted at a station at attention, just outside the delivery room wall, watching to see who and what was coming into the room. He must have been there to keep any dark spirits from entering, because when I walked in, the darkness I had been feeling did not come through that door with me.

The experience had a major impact on my life. Reflecting on it now, I think it had something to do not only with my state of mind at the time, but also with the future of my son. I think Michael has a lot of potential, and I think that he's a very chosen person. Could it be possible that when infants are born, that Satan tries to influence things even at that early stage? I don't know.

I've always personally believed that there are angels and protecting forces out there. There are just too many things that happen that are hard to explain. When you think that a third of the hosts of heaven were cast out with Satan, you realize that that's a lot of people—a lot of evil around us all the time. Heavenly Father wants us to be obedient. That's our first line of defense. But I'm sure he has an army of angels to help us. I can't believe there's only one line of defense. I believe angels are very significant and very real.

Tina, my wife, and I met Ted and Charlene on top of an immense Mayan ruin in the crumbling pre-Columbian Yucatan city of Coba. We had climbed up the steep, partially excavated pyramid on a hot spring day with a few friends, and thought that our little party was completely alone. In fact, perched high above the jungle ceiling, impenetrable except for an occasional pyramid that jutted up through it, we felt a sense of brutal isolation that gave us an inkling of how the first explorers must have felt in that primal landscape.

On the top of that ancient pyramid was a temple made of ornately carved stone. Vestiges of the original paint had survived. We were commenting that the temple had probably been used for human sacrifice. The ritual for a ceremony of that kind in that part of the world generally involved tearing out the victims still-beating heart and rolling the body down the steep side of the pyramid. As our imaginations recreated that grim scenario, which had probably been repeated thousands of times right there on the alter before us, our imaginations running wild, we suddenly heard muffled voices, as if coming to us from another time and dimension.

It was Ted, Charlene, and two of their traveling companions. While we had been struggling up one side of the pyramid, they had been laboring up the opposite side, and were letting their own imaginations run wild on the other side of the top temple.

It was a strange and wonderful way to meet people who would become long-term friends. Tina and I immediately hit it off with Ted and Charlene. We shared a common interest in spiritual things, and talked nonstop all the way back down the pyramid and through the jungle to our rental cars.

Ted grew up the son of a minister of the Church of the Brethren, a sister denomination of the Mennonite church. Much of his boyhood was spent in a remote part of Puerto Rico, where his father had been called to serve as a missionary and minister.

"We were way out in the mountains," explains Ted, "in a valley that was a center for spiritism when we moved there. A lot of mediums lived there, and they had a lot of seances and that sort of thing. My dad had been trained at a standard U.S. seminary, and was completely unprepared for the realm of the supernatural that he encountered. We became quickly exposed to what was very much a part of the life and world view of the indigenous culture. We discovered that there is a dimension of spiritual reality that impacts and interacts with our lives, for good or for ill. For these people, the concept of spirits, angels, and demons was understood to be a common part of life. Of course, it wasn't part of Dad's world view."

Ted's father began to interact with the people in the valley, and soon met a woman who was the main medium in the area. Resistant at first, the woman was touched and attracted by the minister's message.

"For her," explains Ted, "it was a question of power verses power—spiritual reality. It had to be very real, or she wasn't interested. She knew the difference between the powers of darkness and the powers of light. And she knew that she was vulnerable to and subject to powers that were destructive. Dad's ministry was very Biblical in focus, and it's difficult to teach the life and ministry of Jesus without at least acknowledging what for Jesus was very much a part of his life and ministry—the supernatural, miracles, and angels. That was part of Dad's teaching and preaching, although he had not personally been a part of that world. In the process, this woman was converted and became part of the church, and was transformed in a powerful way."

Ted's father's ministry had triggered an increase of spiritual activity in the area. The spiritists in the valley worked to thwart him and his Christian message. When the woman joined his church, they were incensed. After all, she had been the chief medium in the area. They began casting spells and "hexes" on her. Spirits began attacking her house. Furniture mysteriously moved around during the night. Strange noises were heard. She finally asked the minister to come to her house and cast out the evil spirits. Caught in this maelstrom of spiritism, he soon came to believe, on more than a mere intellectual level, in the literal power and influence of angels and demons.

One Sunday, not long after their arrival in the mountain valley, Ted's father was preaching a sermon. Ted was about eight at the time. He was sitting in the small congregation with his mother. Suddenly he became very excited, very agitated.

"My mom was trying to quiet me down, to find out what I was getting so agitated about," he recalls. "She said that I was looking up at my father, but I kept exclaiming something. Finally, she got me quieted down enough to figure out what was going on. I was saying, 'Look at those two big men standing over Dad!'

"Mom was enough of a student of the *Bible* to recognize that I was seeing angels, and to not react and say that I was just seeing things or imagining things. She asked me to describe them. I don't remember a lot of details, just that they were large beings of light standing over Dad as he was preaching. They were sort of hovering over his shoulders, behind and to each side."

The converted spiritist and the others who were spiritually tuned in had been seeing things like this previously. Several of them had made comments like, "Oh, Pastor, the men of light standing over where you were preaching were beautiful!" Of course, he'd just smile and say, "Thank you." At that point, he wasn't sure that he believed what they were talking about.

Even when he came to believe in the reality of these things, he and his family kept them in perspective. Says Ted: "My parents were very clear that we were not to worship angels or become fixated on them. And yet they knew that we shouldn't deny or resist the reality of their presence and activity in our lives. We regarded them as messengers of light that do God's bidding, but we didn't get sidetracked and focus on them."

Although Ted described the angels he saw near his father as men, he can't say, looking back, that they looked like either men or women. "It's almost like that wasn't an issue," he says.

What were they wearing? "Sort of shimmering robes," he explains, "but it was more the power and the light and presence and purity than mere robes. As humans, we are so externally oriented in our natural responses to things. I think there's something about the supernatural dimension that bypasses that and really gets to the core reality. I think that's why John, in the Book of Revelations, struggled to say what he was seeing. It's so hard to put into natural terms what you're seeing in the spiritual realm. What I remember about them is the sense of their light, and power, and purity, and energy—a very radiant energy."

To those with eyes to see them, angels are everywhere present. In a 1968 general conference address, L.D.S. President David O. McKay recalled a meeting he attended as a young missionary:

> *During the progress of the meeting, an elder on his own*
> *initiative arose and said, "Brethren, there are angels in this room."*

Strange as it may seem, the announcement was not startling; indeed, it seemed wholly proper, though it had not occurred to me there were divine beings present. I only knew that I was overflowing with gratitude for the presence of the Holy Spirit.

I was profoundly impressed, however, when President James L. McMurrin, president of the European Mission, arose and confirmed that statement by pointing to one brother sitting just in front of me and saying, "Yes, brethren, there are angels in this room, and one of them is the guardian angel of that young man sitting there," and he designated one who afterward became a patriarch in the Woodruff Stake of the Church, John Young.

Pointing to another elder, he said, "And one is the guardian angel of that young man there," and he singled out one whom I had known from childhood, David Eccles. Tears were rolling down the cheeks of both of these missionaries—not in sorrow or grief, but as an expression of the overflowing Spirit. Indeed, we were all weeping.

The realization that we are loved to the extent that guardian angels attend us is indeed enough to make most people weep. It is also enough to ignite the fires of hope during times of despair. "When at times trouble comes upon us," said Widtsoe, "and we feel almost given up to despair, and think we have been deserted by friends, let us think of the heavenly companions whom God has assigned to us; who, indeed, would reveal themselves to our eyes but for our lack of faith."

I was formally introduced to my own guardian angels in 1992.

I have a friend, Jane, who has always been able to see spirits. By "spirits" I mean people without bodies—or at least people whose bodies most of us can't see. I didn't know this about Jane until she admitted it one night at a lakeside cabin. A group of us had stayed up late talking, and during the conversation, one of our friends said that he had been struggling with a personal problem.

Jane said quietly that the guardian angel sitting next to him would help him get through it.

It was one of those show-stopper comments. Jane was reluctant to say more, but we wouldn't let her off the hook. She finally admitted that when she was in the right frame of mind, and sometimes even when she wasn't, she could see the spirits that came and went with us. We each had at least one, she said. Sometimes new spirits would show up. But we each had had at least one more or less constant guardian angel.

We got together occasionally as a group back then, and almost always ended up talking about spiritual things. Jane said that certain spirit beings came to the group whenever we met. They were there for the group as a whole, rather than for specific individuals.

That was all Jane told us that night, and she was reticent to talk about it afterwards. But on another night several years later, Tina and I were talking with Jane and a friend named Susanne in our living room. Susanne was in the middle of a devastating divorce, and perhaps because she needed all the support she could get, she asked Jane if a guardian spirit was with her. Jane said there was.

Susanne asked who it was. Jane stared intensely at a spot on the sofa beside her, slightly squinting her eyes. "It's a man," she said after a half minute or so.

Susanne asked if she knew who it was.

Squinting again at the same spot, Jane cocked her head slightly to the side, as people do when they don't quite hear something. "Ed— ... *something*" she said finally. "Not Edward ... *Edmund.* Yes, it's Edmund."

Turning back to us, she explained that she could not "hear" as well as she could "see." Then she told us that the spirit guide seemed to be one of Susanne's deceased relatives.

This consoled Susanne. In fact, the moment she heard it, a look of hope settled on her face that wasn't there before.

There was a pause in the conversation while Susanne soaked this in. The temptation was too much for Tina to resist. She asked Jane if she had a guardian angel, too. Jane said she did. She said she thought it was one of Tina's ancestors. His name was Spencer, though she couldn't tell whether that was a first or last name.

Like it or not, it was my turn next. I wasn't sure I wanted to know if I had a guardian angel. But Tina and Susanne wanted me to know and asked Jane on my behalf. As she had done with the others, Jane concentrated, staring at a particular spot beside me. Then she shifted to the other side. Then above me. Then all around me. When she finally unsquinted her eyes, she looked at me and laughed. "My!" she said, "There's a whole camp of angels around you!"

My first thought was that I was in trouble. Why did I have a whole platoon of angels when Susanne and Tina only had one? The line from the old song, "Swing Low Sweet Chariot" came immediately to mind—the one that goes, "... a band of angels, coming after me, coming for to carry me home." I didn't want to be carried home. I was quite comfortable where I was.

My fears evaporated when Jane described these guides. She said that two of them appeared to be from India or thereabouts. Another was a small oriental man. And another seemed to be an Arab by the way he was dressed. There was also a Native American. She sensed that these were all holy men. In addition—and it was a big addition—there was a huge, dark, physically powerful man. She explained that he was there to protect me.

Rounding out the group was the only female in the camp. Jane's voice became very tender when she told me about her. This woman had been a nun, and had been with me at least as long as Jane had known me, although she had never mentioned it. Jane said that we had loved and watched out for each other since long before this life. She said that our bonds were too close and deep to be expressed in words.

My camp of angels was obviously no disembodied death squad. I knew exactly what it was, and I was thrilled, though surprised. You see, earlier that very week I made a commitment to begin gathering information for a book about spirituality and mysticism. I knew that this quest would require a lot of continued research and personal explorations. Eventually, I knew it would take me into strange and potentially dangerous territories, both spiritually and physically. Having made the commitment, I asked for confirmation that what I was planning to do was right for me to be doing. I was expecting, or at least hoping for confirmation in the form of a warm, fuzzy feeling—certainly nothing as spectacular as a personal introduction to a camp full of angels.

Jane's disclosure not only confirmed my commitment, but blessed it.

Susanne and Tina ran a check on their guardian spirits. Susanne called her father later that night and found that she did, in fact, have a fairly close ancestor (a great-grandfather, I recall) by the name of Edmund. Tina also made a call, and discovered that there were several Spencers in her Grandmother MacGregor's branch of the family tree.

For my own part, there was no way I could check out the guardian spirits I had been introduced to. But I didn't have to. What Jane said felt good. It felt real. I do not believe that I am gullible about spiritual things. I do not accept everything with blind faith. I have heard things said and seen things done, under the guise of goodness and truth, that I rejected as dark and false. But this was not one of them. That night I *did* believe that I was surrounded by angels. And I have never doubted it since.

As much as I'd like to end this part of our discussion on that warm note, my conscience forces me to reveal a "fly in the ointment" that I found during my search through Mormon literature. I came upon it just when I was beginning to feel good about having at last found a concensus of opinion on at least one issue: whether we all have guardian angels. You will remember that Brigham Young said clearly that we do. Other church authorities either agreed with him or at least did not disagree. Everyone seemed to be rolling along in harmonious agreement.

Then I looked up "guardian angels" in Bruce R. McConkie's *Mormon Doctrine*, a book which has been leaned on heavily since its first publication in 1958 as a sort of encyclopedia of accepted L.D.S. theology. Not only did this scholar and apostle state that we do *not* all have guardian angels, but he claimed that statements referring to guardian angels are either figurative or refer to special instances of miraculous protection that may have nothing to do with angels. He writes:

> *There is an old and false sectarian tradition to the effect that all men—or if not that, at least the righteous —have guardian angels, heavenly beings of some sort who attend them and exercise some sort of preserving and guarding care. It is true that there are many specific instances in which angels, by special assignment, have performed particular works whereby faithful people have been guarded and preserved ... But to suppose that either all men or all righteous men have heavenly beings acting as guardians for them runs counter to the basic revealed facts relative to the manner in which the Lord exercises his benevolent watchfulness over his mortal children ... Expressions of patriarchs or others relative to guardian angels must be interpreted either as figurative statements or as utterances having reference to special instances of guarding care of a miraculous nature, instances comparable to Daniel's experience in the lion's den.*

Reading this upset me. "Here is an apostle who died not too long ago," I thought, "a man who continues to be one of the most accepted and quoted arbiters of church theology. How could he publish a statement that was so blatantly contradictory to what other church leaders have said?"

When Brigham Young said, "All people have their guardian angels," how could McConkie call that notion "an old and false sectarian tradition"? When David O. McKay—also a prophet and president of the church—told the church membership about a meeting in which specific guardian angels were identified, how could McConkie claim that references to guardian angels are merely "figurative statements" or "special instances of guarding care of a miraculous nature"?

Shouldn't leaders of the same church agree on such fundamental points of theology as guardian angels?

Yes, I was upset. For about a minute. Then it hit me: "Why *should* they agree? Why should everyone in a church have the same opinion about spiritual things?"

Diversity is healthy. It's *sameness* that is frightening. Diversity of opinion proves that people are out there searching, questioning, spiritually alive. It shows that they have the freedom they need to travel their own personal paths to God.

Where there is a strict unity of opinion, on the other hand, there is cause for alarm. It implies that someone at the top is exercising an unhealthy amount of doctrinal control. It suggests that the control is so strong that the people have either buckled under and suppressed any conflicting opinions, or that they have surrendered to the comfort of toeing the party line, abdicating their right and responsibility to grapple for a personal knowledge of God. In either case, the results are damning.

That's why I couldn't be upset with McConkie's conflicting opinion on the matter of guardian angels for very long. That's why I changed my mind and applauded rather than condemned it. I don't agree with it. But I love what it means. It means that no hierarchical committee combed through *Mormon Doctrine* and said, "You can't write that! You can't think that! It doesn't fit. It's not what *we* believe. It will confuse our members." It means that the people in charge had enough faith in God and in the body of the saints to let them think, ponder, and be challenged.

I believe that Joseph Smith would neither have censored McConkie's divergent opinion nor censured the man for having it. From what I have read about Joseph, he would have listened with intense interest, searched for any truth he could find in it, and then shared his own experiences and knowledge regarding the matter. There's a wonderful account, recorded in the *Documentary History of the Church of Jesus Christ of Latter-day Saints*, that illustrates how the church's founder regarded doctrinal opinions. Joseph, speaking to a congregation of church members, said:

> *Elder Pelatiah Brown, one of the wisest old heads we have among us, and whom I now see before me, has been preaching concerning the beast which was full of eyes before and behind; and for this he was hauled up for trial before the High Council.*
>
> *I did not like the old man being called up for erring in doctrine. It looks too much like the Methodist, and not like the Latter-day Saints. Methodists have creeds which a man must believe or be asked out of their church. I want the liberty of thinking and believing as I please. It feels so good not to be trammeled. It does not prove that a man is not a good man because he errs in doctrine.*
>
> *The High Council undertook to censure and correct Elder Brown, because of his teachings in relation to the beasts. Whether they actually corrected him or not, I am a little doubtful, but don't care.*

The prophet went on to elucidate his own thoughts on the matter. Then, instead of condemning Elder Brown to hell as an apostate, lightly said, "... you missed it that time, old gentleman."

Here was a prophet and church leader who had gazed into heaven repeatedly. Was he threatened by theological beliefs that differed from his own? No. Was he concerned that erring opinions would destroy the souls of those who held them? Obviously not. Did he think that the church would crumble if its members disagreed on doctrinal issues? If he did, he didn't seem to care.

After all, it was not mere opinions that Joseph wanted for his people—it was that brilliant glimpse of heaven, that illuminating glance into eternity that would elevate their knowing beyond the realm of words and definitions. Everything short of that was little more than blind gropings ... and who would condemn a blind man for claiming that an elephant is very much like a rope?

Chapter 5
Why Does God Need Angels Anyway?

"He [God] sends angels and ministering spirits to transact His business, upon the same principle that brother Brigham sends his brethren to England, Denmark, the States, and this way, and that. He sits upon His throne and says, Joseph, go and do that; Peter, attend to that; and they do it. This is a natural principle there just as much as here ... "

— *Heber C. Kimball*, Journal of Discourses

If God is all-knowing and all-powerful, why does he need angels to help get things done?

A little boy is drowning in an icy lake. It's not his time to die. Surely God himself could pluck him out of the water. To deny that he could would be to deny his omnipotence. So why would he need to send an angel to do the job?

Perhaps the answer lies not so much in what God can or cannot do, but in what angels *need* to do for their spiritual progress, or what they *want* to do for those they love. In other words, maybe God doesn't need angels at all. Maybe angels need the opportunity to serve.

There is a tendency to think that when people die, they pass directly into a realm of heavenly bliss where there is no more spiritual progress, and where they leave all their earthly affections and attachments behind. Mormon theology holds that this is far from true. Mormons believe that earthly death is something like a change of assignment—that we go on progressing as spirit beings; that we carry with us, like chains or wings, the attachments and love we had in mortality. What better way to progress than to serve as angels; and whom better to serve than those we love and leave behind?

My wife tells me that when her father was close to death, faced with leaving a wife and six young children behind, he told them that he would be able to help them more from the other side than he was able to here on earth. Several of them, including Tina, today attest that he has in fact been busy helping them since he passed away. During his life, certain circumstances prevented him from doing everything he wanted to do for his children as a father. His loving service from the other side has surely allowed him to fulfill much—if not all—of those desires. As my own son's experience affirms, he has even been busy as a grandfather.

The idea that angelic ministrations are more for angels than for God, logical as it may seem, is disputed by some who think that there are, in fact, some things that angels can do that God *can't* do.

Wilford Woodruff, the fourth president of the L.D.S. Church, had this to say:

> One of the Apostles said to me years ago, "Brother Woodruff, I have prayed for a long time for the Lord to send the administration of an angel to me. I have had a great desire for this, but I have never had my prayers answered."
>
> I said to him that if he were to pray a thousand years to the God of Israel for that gift it would not be granted, unless the Lord had a motive in sending an angel to him. I told him that the Lord never did nor never will send an angel to anybody merely to gratify the desire of the individual to see an angel. If the Lord sends an angel to anyone, He sends him to perform a work that cannot be performed only by the administration of an angel. I said to him that these were my views.

The Lord had sent angels to men from the creation of the world, at different times, but always with a message or with something to perform that could not be performed without.

Here, President Woodruff speaks of works that "cannot be performed only by the administration of an angel," which implies that even God can't perform them, for some reason or another. He also admits that this is only his view, which is comforting to those who would have a difficult time accepting the notion that there are things God can't do. But if what he says is true, then the services angels perform become an indispensable cog in the machinery of the universe—a cog that God himself cannot do without.

Early Mormon apostle Orson Hyde concurs with this view. He said:

> *The Lord is everywhere present by His ministering angels, just like any other ruler, monarch or king, who has ministers everywhere throughout His dominions; and God's ministers are everywhere; He has servants tabernacled in flesh on earth, and they are going through the land in every direction, and God is present everywhere with them; and He knows everything. How? When His angels and ministers tell Him of it, like any other ruler ... God knows everything through His agents, or servants, and that is the way He is everywhere present.*

Jean-Jacques Rousseau, the 18th-century Swiss-French philosopher, scoffed at the idea that God is in any way "like any other ruler" and that his omnipresence depends on angels, as Hyde claimed. "A very pretty device, truly, is that of the angel!" he wrote sarcastically. "Not contented with subjecting us to this angelic hierarchy, they would reduce even the Deity himself to the necessity of employing it."

Joseph Fielding Smith, the eleventh president of the L.D.S. church, found a middle way between these conflicting opinions. While affirming God's omnipotence, he focused on the idea that there exists a "true order of communication" between God and man which can include intercession by both God *and* angels. He wrote:

> *No one can be more free to admit his [God's] perfect right and power to visit whom he pleases, at his pleasure, for the channels of communication between God and man cannot be cut off nor closed by man, nor ever will be while God has a purpose to accomplish by revealing himself ... God has instituted the true order of communication between himself and man ... It is in perfect harmony with the order of heaven for ministering spirits or messengers from God or Christ to visit the Lamanites or any other people ...*

Mormon leader and scholar James E. Talmage also hit this middle ground when he wrote ...

> *God is Omniscient—By Him matter has been organized and energy directed. He is therefore the Creator of all things that are created; and "Known unto God are all his works from the beginning of the world." His power and His wisdom are alike incomprehensible to man, for they are infinite. Being Himself eternal and perfect, His knowledge cannot be otherwise than infinite. To comprehend Himself, an infinite Being, He must possess an infinite mind. Through the agency of angels and ministering servants He is in continuous communication with all parts of creation, and may personally visit as He may determine.*

Again we ask: Does God really need angels? And if so, why? It would be nice to be able to find final, definitive answers. But we can't. Like so many other questions regarding angels, they are probably not likely to be answered fully and incontestably until they are answered in our individual hearts when the time is right.

Until then, we are just blind men touching the elephant.

Chapter 6
Angels of Death and Destruction
... Somebody's Got to Do It

And the four angels were loosed, which were prepared for an hour, and a day, and a month, and a year, for to slay the third part of men. — Revelation 9:15

Imagine this: You're an angel, and you're standing in line waiting to get your next job assignment. The angel two ahead of you gets up to the desk and is told to go down and watch over little Tyler Jones, a newborn who is going to grow up and develop a safe, environmentally friendly energy source. The angel just ahead of you is told to go help a small group of people who are trying to raise funds to build orphanages in Latin America.

You approach the desk, wondering who you're going to be asked to help, whose life you're going to have the opportunity to save, what good cause you're going to be able to advance.

"So what's it going to be?" you ask excitedly. "What's my assignment?"

"Let's see," says the official behind the desk. "Oh, yes. Here it is. It looks like you and the next three angels in line will be wiping out a third of the human race. Here's a packet with all the details, and you can pick up the equipment you'll need in the armory. Have a nice day."

Levity aside, you have to wonder about the less appetizing of the angelic duties—death and destruction, for example. If we are to take Revelation 9:15 literally, four angels are going to wipe out a third of the human race. That definitely qualifies as a less appetizing assignment, at least from our perspective. It doesn't sound at all "angelic." But that particular task, though perhaps larger in scope than most, is certainly not unique in its nature. Angels of death and destruction, and what they do, are frequently mentioned in the scriptures and spoken of by Mormon leaders. Here are just a few of the many references on the subject:

> *It was in the family of Geo. W. Therlkill also that the angel of death struck down his first victim in the valley. A child three years old, a boy, playing on the banks of City Creek fell in and was drowned. His body was found in the creek about 5 p. m. of the 11th of August. The occurrence threw a gloom over the colony, which President Young sought to dispel on the following Sunday by a discourse on the sureness of the salvation of children.*
> — *B.H. Roberts*, Comprehensive History of the Church

> *No man can stop the work of the Lord, for God rules the pestilence, and the pestilence rules men. Forts, sentinels, and oceans may hinder men, or money may bribe, but when the pestilence rides on the wings of the wind, the sentinel has no power; the fort is no obstacle, the ocean is no barrier, and money has no value, the destroying angel goes waving the banner of death over all; and who shall escape his pointed arrow?*
> — *Joseph Smith*, History of the Church

> *The day that we landed the destroying angel visited our camp, and, of course, there was sorrow. I do not know the number that went to the grave, but somewhere about fourteen, I think.*
> — *Wilford Woodruff*, Collected Discourses

Therefore, as the time draws near when the sun is to be darkened, the moon turn to blood, and the stars fall from heaven, the Lord will bring to the knowledge of his people his commandments and statutes, that they may be prepared to stand when the earth shall reel to and fro as a drunken man, earthquakes cause the nations to tremble, and the destroying angel goes forth to waste the inhabitants at noon day ...   — Times and Seasons, Volume 2

The angel of death cuts one short of mortal life for disobedience; the angel of light makes the way clear for the spiritual life eternal.
    — *Spencer W. Kimball*, The Miracle of Forgiveness

From this promise in the Word of Wisdom and other scriptures, it appears that there are destroying angels who have a work to do among the peoples of the earth in this last dispensation. The Lord told the Prophet Joseph Smith that because all flesh was corrupted before him, and the powers of darkness prevailed upon the earth, these angels were waiting the great command to reap down the earth, to gather the tares that they may be burned.
    — Marion G. Romney, Conference Report, 1952

Clearly, these angels of death and destruction are more than mere symbols of natural events. They are literal beings performing literal works. Wilford Woodruff drives this point home with a story from his missionary days:

... there were some fifteen or twenty deaths during my stay there. Men were taken with what was called pleurisy. Doctors came in and opened a vein, and they died in five minutes. One of these men sent for me, and I went and saw him. Two men were holding him. He said to me, "I wish you would cut open my side; I have a pain here and it is skin deep; you can cut it out and save my life." I looked at him, but did not say anything to him. I said to

myself, "If your eyes were open, you would see the angel of death standing by your side." He died while I was there.

Make no mistake: we are not talking about the dark side here. These are not bad angels doing evil deeds. They are *good* angels doing *good* deeds—acts that need to be performed; things that are just and right from an eternal perspective, even though they may appear dark and sinister from our limited points of view.

There is no reason to assume that angels of death and destruction look different than other angels of light, or that they radiate a dark, threatening energy. Some religious and cultural systems would have us believe that they do, however. I know a devout man who is a practicing sihk. He claims to have had personal encounters with the angel of death. He describes this being as looking somewhat like Darth Vader in *Star Wars*. The angel's black aura, he says, unfurls like a billowing, Dracula-style cape as he stretches his arms out to envelop the dying person in a cold embrace and wrest him from this world, actually pulling his soul out of his body. He says that this final embrace is so terrifying that we remember it with horror from one life to the next. That, he explains, is why death is mankind's greatest fear.

The Christian concept and experience of death is far more benign. We believe that instead of being enveloped and carried off in stark terror by a horrific angel, the dying are more likely to be visited by loving angels and escorted into the light and glory of the next phase of existence. These angels of death, if indeed they can be called that, are often family members or other individuals who were dear to them. Consequently, the time of dying is not one of fear and dread, but of peace and joy.

Good-night, sweet prince,
And flight of angels sing thee to thy rest!
— *William Shakespeare,* Hamlet

That has been the experience in my own family. My great-great-grandfather, James Allred, served as a bodyguard to Joseph Smith, whom he revered. My grandfather was at the side of the old patriarch when he died long after the martyrdom of his beloved prophet. He said that the elderly gentleman suddenly opened his eyes and stared intensely at a point near the upper edge of the opposite wall. Stretching out one hand as if to clutch at another, he raised himself up off the bed and exclaimed, "Joseph! Joseph!" Then a look of ineffable bliss spread over his face as he sank back peacefully and gave up the ghost.

My grandfather—the one who was present during that incident—died in his 80s in a hospital room. During the moments of his death, he was alone with my grandmother. As his spirit left him, she embraced him, and she told my mother later that they were enveloped for several minutes in a feeling of love more sweet and intense than she had ever felt in her life.

When my grandmother died, my mother was with her in her small rural home. She was walking from the kitchen into the living room when she slumped over and fell to the floor. She died as peacefully as a child falls asleep. My mother told me that she will never forget the feeling of love and peace that descended over her as she held that wonderful woman in her arms as her spirit passed to the next world.

Certainly, no terrifying angels of death were present in any of these instances. The angels in attendance, whether they could officially be designated as angels of death or not, must have been beautiful both in appearance and in the energy they radiated. Perhaps this is not always the case. I'm sure there are those who die kicking, screaming, and dragging their deathbed sheets with them. But even then, I would think that their reluctance to leave this life could be blamed more on attachments to worldly things than on the appearance of a Darth Vader look-alike from the realm of spirits.

So much for angels of death. But what about angels of destruction? My search for personal references or experiences involving angels of destruction—what they look like, what it feels like to be in their presence, and so forth—yielded nothing. But that's to be expected. When these angels are doing their work, people are probably too busy being destroyed to take notes about their appearance, if they see them at all. Those that do see them probably don't survive to tell about it.

And so we'll leave this unpleasant though important facet of the angel phenomenon with this piece of advice: Don't be too anxious to know more about angels of death and destruction. If and when the time comes to meet one, you won't mistake its touch. It will likely be the last.

Chapter 7
Dark Angels —
The Other Side of Light

I think it is the weakness of mine eyes
That shapes this monstrous apparition.
It comes upon me. Art thou any thing?
Art thou some god, some angel, or some devil,
That makest my blood cold and my hair to stare!
Speak to me what thou art.
—*William Shakespeare*, Julius Caesar

Ron and his missionary companion were working in an obscure village in the Guatemala highlands. I was stationed in the capital of El Salvador at the time, which was part of the same Mormon mission back then. During a conference in Guatemala City, I had a chance to talk to Ron. We had been friends since our stint in the Missionary Training Center together. He told me about something that happened just a few weeks before.

It was during one of the area's most festive religious holidays: *Semana Santa*. Unable to get any missionary work done, Ron and his companion were playing ping-pong one night in a small room in the building they used as a chapel. There had been two different parades that day, one sponsored by the local Catholic hierarchy, the other by one of the evangelical churches. Booths, tables, and blankets had been set up along the streets by witches and shamans selling blessings, curses, amulets, and cure-alls. These were talismans of the Guatemalan style of voodoo—a melding of traditional Mayan religious practice with the more recent theological imports. The whole thing, said Ron, was a spiritual free-for-all that left him and his companion feeling dark and uneasy.

The room was dimly lit and only large enough to accommodate the ping-pong table and give the players a little elbow room. The doorway to the room was situated directly behind where Ron stood playing. It opened into a dark hallway. As they were playing, something odd happened. Ron's companion hit the ball off the table, and instead of following its line of trajectory into the corner of the room, it changed courses as it bounced—as if pulled by an invisible magnet—and rolled out into the hall. Thinking that his companion had put some kind of strange spin on the ball, Ron grabbed it and resumed playing.

A few minutes later, the same thing happened, except this time the change of direction was too radical to be attributed to any kind of spin. Ron stepped out into the dark hall and reached down for the ball, but it kept bouncing away from his grasp. Suddenly he felt an evil presence in the hall. Abandoning the ball, he turned and lunged for the door. Just as he crossed the threshold, he felt three quick draughts of ice-cold air brush the back of his neck in rapid succession. The deathly air, he said, was almost palpable. He was afraid to look back. Instead, he looked ahead and saw his companion standing frozen and wide-eyed on the other side of the table. The companion was not looking at Ron but into the hallway.

Ron dropped his mallet and walked quickly around the table. Both missionaries backed up to the wall and stood looking through the doorway for several minutes, terrified and speechless. Finally, Ron asked his companion what he had seen. He said that he saw a hand reach out from the darkness of the hallway just as Ron plunged back into the room. The hand, he said, took three swipes at the back of Ron's neck, as if to grab him. Later, Ron's companion described the hand as something black—something darker than the darkness surrounding it.

───── ⁂ ─────

"The devil is an angel too."
— *Miguel de Unamuno*, Two Mothers

This is not a light story. But then, not all stories that involve other-worldly beings are light. Some—many—are dark. Dark as hell.

There are dark, demonic angels. These are not good angels that do unpleasant things for the right reasons, as we discussed in the previous chapter. No, these are the bad guys of the cosmos. There are no good intentions about them. If they could tear God into microscopic pieces and bury those pieces forever in a far corner of the universe, they would. If they could lure you into the realm of black suffering and laugh at your screams and tears throughout eternity, they would.

In my search for angels, it was not my intention to find anything dark. But it was inevitable that I should. In this world of opposites, the closer you get to the light, the more the darkness reaches out to grab you.

When the Church of Jesus Christ of Latter-Day Saints was emerging in the early 1800s, Satan and his angels knew that God was upping the ante of light and truth in the world. It was therefore not surprising that the powers of darkness worked overtime to stop it. Consequently, the early members of the Mormon church were well versed in angels and demons alike—and not just from a theoretical point of view. Like Jacob of the Old Testament, who wrestled with an angel all night long, many of these people had hands-on experience with diverse types of otherworldly beings. This account, told by Heber C. Kimball, one of the church's first great missionaries and apostles, is indicative of the kinds of things that went on:

Perhaps there are some who do not believe much in spirits, but I know that they exist and visit the earth, and I will tell you how and why I know it. When I was in England, brother Geo. D. Watt was the first man baptized, and his mother was baptized directly after he was. The night previous to my going forward to baptize brother Watt and eight others, I had a vision, as old father Baker used to say, "of the infernal world."

I saw legions of wicked spirits that night, as plain as I now see you, and they came as near to me as you now are, and company after company of them rushed towards me; and brother Hyde and brother Richards also saw them. It was near the break of day, and I looked upon them as I now look upon you. They came when I was laying hands upon brother Russell, the wicked spirits got him to the door of the room, I did not see them till after that took place, and soon afterwards I lay prostrate upon the floor ... That was the first introduction of the Gospel into England, and I was shown those spirits as plainly as ever I saw anything ...

If evil spirits could come to me, cannot ministering spirits and angels also come from God? Of course they can, and there are thousands of them, and I wish you to understand this, and that they can rush as an army going to battle, for the evil spirits came upon me and brother Hyde in that way. There is one circumstance in the visit of those evil spirits, that I would not tell if brother Hyde had not often told it himself; they spoke and said to brother Hyde, "We have nothing against you," no, but I was the lad that they were after.

I mention this to show that the devil is an enemy to me, he is also an enemy to brother Brigham, to brother Jedediah, to the Twelve, and to every righteous man. When brother Benson goes to the old country he will find hosts of evil spirits, and he will know more about the devil than he ever did before. The spirits of the wicked, who have died for thousands of years past, are at war with the Saints of God upon the earth. Do I ever pray that I may see them again? No, I do not. We had prayed all day, and almost all night, that we might have power to establish the Gospel in England. Previous to this, Mr. Fielding, a clergyman, came and forbid my baptizing those persons who had come forward. Said I, sir, they are of age, and I shall baptize them, if they wish for it, and I baptized nine. The next morning I was so weak that I could scarcely stand, so great was the effect that those spirits had upon me ...

When I returned home I called upon bother Joseph [Smith], and we walked down the bank of the river. He there told me what contests he had had with the devil; he told me that he had contests with the devil, face to face. He also told me how he was handled and afflicted by the devil, and said, he had known circumstances where Elder Rigdon was pulled out of bed three times in one night.

(Journal of Discourses, Vol. 3.)

Dey's two angels hoverin' roun' 'bout him. One uv 'em is white en shiny, en 'tother one is black. De white one gits him to go right, a little while, den de black one sail in en bust it all up. A body can't tell, yit, which one gwyne to fetch him at de las'.

—Mark Twain, *The Adventures of Huckleberry Finn*

We know who the Devil is. But who are *angels of the Devil?* Without flipping back into my scholar mode and trying to pin down the un-pin-downable, allow me to have a quick go at answering that question in at least a general sense.

At least some of these bad guys are who we might call evil "ghosts." We just read Heber C. Kimball's statement. "The spirits of the wicked," he said, "who have died for thousands of years past, are at war with the Saints of God upon the earth." So, some of these dark angels are nothing more or less than people like us who have lived here, didn't do too well in the spiritual sense, and are still hanging around playing havoc. They are literally "damned" in that their desires are keeping them from moving on. Whether they are bitterly trying to bring others down to their level, or hanging around trying to make life miserable for the person who stole their spouse, or sitting in the darkness of pornographic movie theaters trying to douse their lust without a body to douse it with, they are trapped and held captive by their own carnal desires.

"Many spirits of the departed, who are unhappy, linger in lonely wretchedness about the earth, and in the air, and especially about their ancient homesteads, and the places rendered dear to them by the memory of former scenes," explains Parley P. Pratt in *Key to the Science of Theology*. "The more wicked of these are the kind spoken of in Scripture, as 'foul spirits,' 'unclean spirits,' spirits who afflict persons in the flesh, and engender various diseases in the human system. They will sometimes enter human bodies, and will distract them, throw them into fits, cast them into the water, into the fire, etc. They will trouble them with dreams, nightmares, hysterics, fever, etc. They will also deform them in body and in features, by convulsions, cramps, contortions, etc., and will sometimes compel them to utter blasphemies, horrible curses, and even words of other languages. If permitted, they will often cause death. Some of these spirits are adulterous, and suggest to the mind all manner of lasciviousness, all kinds of evil thoughts and temptations."

In short, these are not happy campers. And it appears that they are trying to throw major monkey wrenches into the lives of the rest of us. One of the many ways they do this, according to Brigham Young, is to give us false revelations. He once said of certain people who claimed to belong to a higher order of spiritualism that they received their revelations "from every foul spirit that has departed this life, and gone out of the bodies of mobbers, murderers, highwaymen, drunkards, thieves, liars, and every kind of debauched character, whose spirits are floating around here, and searching and seeking whom they can destroy; for they are the servants of the devil, and they are permitted to come now to reveal to the people."

We also know about another type of dark angel: the third of God's children who decided to throw in with Satan rather than with God and Christ at the great council in heaven before the world began. We have been told that these spiritual brothers and sisters of ours, because of their rebellion, won't be going through this earthly experience with physical bodies, as the rest of us are doing. Consequently, they are bitter and do whatever they can to take over our bodies; or failing that, to send us to hell in a hand basket.

Says George Q. Cannon, an early leader of the Mormon church: "They were not permitted to take tabernacles. They were cast out of heaven—one-third, we are told, of the whole hosts of heaven—and they became angels to the devil; and from that day until the present they have been wandering about in the earth, tempting the children of men, seeking to lead them astray; infusing into their hearts rebellion and disobedience against God, adultery, dishonesty, and vice of every kind, and endeavoring, as the agents of Satan, to bring the rest of the family of God into the same dreadful condition which they now occupy."

You might ask why anyone would be bitter about missing out on an earthly experience that makes us vulnerable to IRS audits and hemorrhoids. But no matter what we go through in this earth-bound state, it is obviously far better than *not* having the experience at all. And so, this rebellious 33 1/3 percent of God's children wage war against him by attacking the other 66 2/3 percent when they come to earth. A little math tells us that the tiny portion of the 66 2/3 percent group that can be found on earth at any given time is vastly outnumbered by the full army of the rebellious third, even taking vacation time and sick leave into account.

This is clearly a force to be taken seriously—especially if you are actively on the side of light. Joseph Smith said, "He that will war the true Christian warfare against the corruptions of these last days will have wicked men and angels of devils, and all the infernal powers of darkness continually arrayed against him."

I should point out that my attempts to try to define angels of the devil met with the same sort of confusion and conflicts of opinion that I encountered when I tried to define good angels. For example, after all that is written about the different categories of dark angels, which we'll discuss in the following pages, we then run headlong into Brigham Young's statement, which reads, "None will become angels to the devil except those who have sinned against the Holy Ghost." He is referring to "sons of perdition"—a much smaller group of people than the others mentioned. Again, so much for trying to define the elephant.

In pride, in reas'ning pride, our error lies;
All quit their sphere, and rush into the skies.
Pride still is aiming at the blest abodes,
Men would be angels, angels would be gods.
Aspiring to be gods, if angels fell,
Aspiring to be angels, men rebel:
And who but wishes to invert the laws
Of order, sins against th' eternal cause.

—*Alexander Pope*

A final general category of dark angels is perhaps the most intriguing and dangerous of all: fallen angels ... a.k.a., good angels gone bad. In the apocryphal *Epistle of Jude*, angels are mentioned who "kept not their own principality, but left their proper habitation ..."

In the days before the great flood, fallen angels stirred up trouble of cosmic proportions. Mormon scholar Hugh Nibley tells us more about these characters in his book, *Enoch the Prophet:*

The wickedness of Enoch's day had a special stamp and flavor; only the most determined and entrenched depravity merited the extermination of the race. In apocryphal Enoch stories we are told how humanity was led to the extremes of misconduct under the tutelage of uniquely competent masters. According to these traditions, these were none other than special heavenly messengers who were sent down to earth to restore respect for the name of God among the degenerate human race but instead yielded to temptation, misbehaved with the daughters of men, and ended up instructing and abetting their human charges in all manner of iniquity. They are variously designated as the Watchers, Fallen Angels, Sons of God, Nephilim, or Rephaim, and are sometimes confused with their offspring, the Giants.

Weird stuff, indeed. Special heavenly messengers coming to earth, having sex with human women, siring giants (which are mentioned several times in the Old Testament), and then teaching humans mysteries that they were not ready to handle. This is the stuff of myth, legend, and action thrillers.

> *Of early nature, and the vigorous race*
> *Of undiseased mankind, the giant sons*
> *Of the embrace of angels with a sex*
> *More beautiful than they, which did draw down*
> *The erring spirits who can ne'er return.*
> — *Lord Byron,* Manfred

Nibley goes on to explain that the situation got so out of hand on earth that men in essence declared war on God. Their actions soon threatened to alter the very order of things not only in this world, but throughout the universe. Writes Nibley: "Characteristics of the sweep and scope of the Enoch apocalyptic are the disturbances of the whole cosmos, for Enoch wept not just for the earth but for the heaven's sake ... This is a common theme in the Enoch literature. The whole cosmos shares the fate of a violated planet."

Other heavenly angels—good guys—seeing the progressive evil on earth, and fearing the threat to the entire universe, petitioned God repeatedly to wipe the earth's slate clean. In what appears to be a palliative measure, "God permitted certain angels to go to the sons of adultery and destroy the sons of the watchers who were among mankind and set them to fighting against each other," says Nibley. Eventually, he points out that even a reluctant God could stay his hand no longer, and called down the great flood.

The idea of mighty angels that come to earth with Godly commissions, but end up doing evil because they succumb to worldly temptations is both intriguing and frightening. It is intriguing in its theological ramifications. It is frightening in its practical implications. Imagine how powerful this kind of fallen angel would be. Knowing most of the deep mysteries, and invulnerable to many of the physical problems and limitations to which the rest of us are prey, these bad guys from heaven could really play hell here. They did before the flood. Could they now?

More specifically, are any of these fallen angels on earth right now? In a way, it would be comforting to blame the evil we see around us on them. On a personal level, I know that when I see, hear, or read about atrocities, something deep inside me is appalled by the thought that such horrors were committed by someone of my own species. If one of my kindred human beings engineered the extermination of six million Jews, then why should I assume that I could not be capable of such a thing under the right set of circumstances? If one of my human brothers can kidnap, rape, and brutally kill a four-year-old child, then—God forbid!—couldn't I, too, be capable of committing such an unspeakable act?

Yes, it would be nice to be able to blame all the world's evils on beings that are not of our species. We can't, of course. But can't we shift at least some of the blame to fallen angels? No one knows for sure. In fact, no one even knows if any of them are around here anymore—no one who is willing to talk about it, that is.

We *do* know, however, that the other categories of dark angels (the rebellious third, and the spirits of the wicked dead) are here, and very active. Misery loves company, and they prod us to do what is contrary to God's laws so that we'll be as miserable as they are. We also know that they have a real hunger for being inside our bodies, and so they try to literally possess us.

Hair-raising stories about dark angels are all too plentiful. Ask almost any missionary. Ask kids or adults who have played with Ouija boards, dabbled in seances, or participated in devil worship of any kind. I will not recount any other dark stories in this book. I agree with C.S. Lewis in *The Screwtape Letters*. He said that the two greatest errors we can commit in relation to the devil are to (1) deny his existence, or (2) give him too much attention. I have admitted his existence. I won't do him the honor of giving him more attention by sensationalizing his grim powers with other spine-tingling accounts.

Dark angels wouldn't be half the trouble they are if they always looked like dark angels. The trouble is, they sometimes masquerade as angels of light to fool us. "The devil, in fact, when he dresses himself in angel's clothes," wrote Samuel Butler in *Way of All Flesh*, "can only be detected by experts of exceptional skill, and so often does he adopt this disguise that it is hardly safe to be seen talking to an angel at all ..."

Joseph Smith spoke of "the false spirits that so frequently are made manifest among the Latter-day Saints." In his *History of the Church*, he described a specific incidence of angelic deception:

> *There have also been ministering angels in the Church which were of Satan appearing as an angel of light. A sister in the state of New York had a vision, who said it was told her that if she would go to a certain place in the woods, an angel would appear to her. She went at the appointed time, and saw a glorious personage descending, arrayed in white, with sandy colored hair; he commenced and told her to fear God, and said that her husband was called to do great things, but that he must not go more than one hundred miles from home, or he would not return; whereas God had called him to go to the ends of the earth, and he has since been more than one thousand miles from home, and is yet alive.*

Many true things were spoken by this personage, and many things that were false. How, it may be asked, was this known to be a bad angel? By the color of his hair; that is one of the signs that he can be known by, and by his contradicting a former revelation.

If bad angels can pose as good angels, how are we supposed to know the difference?

According to the *Falasha Anthology*, Abraham himself had trouble telling the good angels from the bad. "I do not know whether thou art a great angel," said Abraham, when confronted with an other-than-earthly being. "When angels come to me I feel strong, my soul is fortified ... but when thou camest my soul was troubled ... my tongue became heavy and weak."

Certainly, the energy an angel radiates is an excellent clue as to whether or not it is of the light or the dark sort. Parley P. Pratt offers some additional clues:

Spirits are those who have departed this life, and have not yet been raised from the dead. These are of two kinds, viz.—Good and evil. These two kinds also include many grades of good and evil. The good spirits, in the superlative sense of the word, are they who, in this life, partook of the Holy Priesthood, and of the fullness of the Gospel. This class of spirits minister to the heirs of salvation, both in this world and in the world of spirits. They can appear unto men, when permitted; but not having a fleshly tabernacle, they can not hide their glory. Hence, an unembodied spirit, if it be a holy personage, will be surrounded with a halo of resplendent glory, or brightness, above the brightness of the sun.

Whereas, spirits not worthy to be glorified will appear without this brilliant halo; and although they often attempt to pass as angels of light, there is more or less of darkness about them ...

A person on looking another in the eye, who is possessed of an evil spirit, may feel a shock, a nervous feeling, which will, as it were, make his hair stand on end, in short, a shock resembling that produced in a nervous system by the sight of a serpent.

Some of these foul spirits, when possessing a person, will cause a disagreeable smell about the person thus possessed, which will be plainly manifest to the senses of those about him, even though the person thus afflicted should be washed and change his clothes every few minutes.

Joseph Smith and his religious contemporaries were often confronted by beings from the spirit world, both good and evil, including the devil. "We may look for angels and receive their ministrations," said Joseph, "but we are to try the spirits and prove them, for it is often the case that men make a mistake in regard to these things ... Lying spirits are going forth in the earth. There will be great manifestations of spirits, both false and true."

So frequent were these encounters with both heavenly and hellish beings, and so difficult it was at times to distinguish the one type from the other, that Joseph asked the Lord for help. The tips he was given are recorded in the *Doctrine and Covenants* (129:4–9):

When a messenger comes saying he has a message from God, offer him your hand and request him to shake hands with you. If he be an angel he will do so, and you will feel his hand. If he be the spirit of a just man made perfect he will come in his glory; for that is the only way he can appear—Ask him to shake hands with you, but he will not move, because it is contrary to the order of heaven for a just man to deceive; but he will still deliver his message. If it be the devil as an angel of light, when you ask him to shake hands he will offer you his hand, and you will not feel anything; you may therefore detect him. These are three grand keys whereby you may know whether any administration is from God.

That's all well and fine for people who are well acquainted with angels. But I know that if I saw an angel—good or bad—I doubt I'd be thinking clearly enough to subject him to the handshake test. I probably wouldn't be thinking at all. Chances are I'd be running in the opposite direction screaming.

There is a way to put the devil on the run, though this too requires a certain amount of self-control and presence of mind. Joseph Smith revealed it when he described a way to discern the difference between an angel of light and the devil himself. "The devil may appear as an angel of light," he explained. "Ask God to reveal it; if it be of the devil, he will flee from you; if of God, He will manifest Himself, or make it manifest."

For Joseph, these words of instruction were more than academic. He had actually been confronted by the devil masquerading as an angel of light. In Section 128 of the *Doctrine and Covenants*, he refers to the "voice of Michael on the banks of the Susquehanna, detecting the devil when he appeared as an angel of light!"

One last note before we leave this subject of dark angels. Even though those of us living on the earth at any given time in the flesh are far outnumbered by the dark angels we have identified in this chapter, our team is heavily favored to win. In a talk given in Salt Lake City in 1856, Mormon apostle Heber C. Kimball explains why: "... some persons will say to me, that there are no evil spirits. I tell you they are thicker than the 'Mormons' are in this country, but the Lord has said that there are more for us than there can be against us. 'Who are they,' says one? Righteous men who have been upon the earth ...

"Do you suppose that there are any angels here today?" continues Kimball. "I would not wonder if there were ten times more angels here than people. We do not see them, but they are here watching us, and are anxious for our salvation."

Chapter 8
When Angels Help . . .
and When They Don't

Matthew, Mark, Luke, and John,
The bed be blest that I lie on.
Four angels to my bed,
Four angels round my head,
One to watch, and one to pray,
And two to bear my soul away.
— Thomas Ady, A Candle in the Dark

A friend of ours, Tammy, had to have a hysterectomy — the kind that required no incision. Everything went fine, and the nurses put her to bed for the night. She was to be released the next morning after the doctor removed the packing.

To help her get a good night's sleep, a nurse gave Tammy a pain pill. "Those sorts of pills really knock me out," she admits. "I was sound asleep."

Tammy's father had passed away the year before. "He had a way of waking me up when I was a little girl when I'd fall asleep on the couch," she recalls fondly. "He was a tease. He'd sort of torture me by saying, 'Come on, Tammy, come on, you've got to get up, let's go, come on, time to get up, let's get going …' He'd keep it up until

I'd get so mad that I'd literally get up swinging. It was his way of teasing. He loved to see me jump up half asleep like a wild little animal.

"So there I was, sound asleep in the hospital room at about two in the morning, on pain pills that had really knocked me out, and I started hearing a voice saying, 'Get up, get up, come on Tammy, you've got to get up, come on, let's go, get up ...'

"I remember trying to wake up, but I couldn't because I was so out of it. I remember mumbling 'I can't ... I'm sleepy.' But the voice kept saying 'Get up! Come on Tammy, get up!' It was insistent. It just kept at it.

"Finally I got mad—just like I used to—and I woke up and yelled, *What? What is it?*' I sat up in the dark room, and of course, no one else was there. But I felt wet—wet all over. And the bed was wet. I staggered to the bathroom, feeling really woozy, turned on the light, and saw that I was covered with blood from head to toe! I was hemorrhaging."

Tammy buzzed the nurses. They came in, took one look at her, and immediately started emergency procedures. Doctors and nurses worked feverishly and saved her life. But what *really* saved her that night was the voice that anxiously teased her awake in the quiet of a dark hospital room.

As it happened, the doctor had nipped an artery during the surgery earlier that day, but no one was aware of it because of the packing. If she hadn't been awakened when she was, she would have been dead ... probably within a few more minutes.

Although Tammy remembers that the voice was very distinct, she can't say that it was her father's voice. "I can't even say whether it was a male or female voice," she admits. "It was just a voice. But it was just the way Dad used to tease me awake when I was a little girl. If the voice wasn't my dad's, I think he had a part in telling someone, 'This is the way you're going to have to wake her up.'

"Even my doctor tells this story now. I remember he asked me after it happened, 'What woke you up?' And I said, 'I think it was my dad.' It was bizarre, but it was real. It really did occur. Some things you can't explain. Obviously, somebody felt the need to save me.

"I guess it wasn't my time to go."

———————※※※———————

"Their garments are white, but with an unearthly whiteness. I cannot describe it, because it cannot be compared to earthly whiteness; it is much softer to the eye. These bright Angels are enveloped in a light so different from ours that by comparison everything else seems dark. When you see a band of fifty, you are lost in amazement. They seem clothed with golden plates, constantly moving, like so many suns." — Pere Lamy

At the age of 17, Julia came only inches from willfully throwing her own life away. But it wasn't her time to go, either. She had been living in New York City since she was 15 years old, attending the prestigious School of American Ballet, under the direction of George Balanchine. "I was the best in my class," she explains, "which meant that I would be put into the New York City Ballet, in the apprenticeship program. But that was the year Mikhail Baryshnikov joined the New York City Ballet, and Baryshnikov was very short and I'm very tall.

"When I went in for my evaluation, Balanchine said, 'Julie, you're a very good dancer, but I need short girls to stand next to Baryshnikov.' So he hired all short girls that year, and I was left out in the cold. I had been doing *everything* to become a New York City Ballet dancer."

Crushed, the teenage girl returned to her boarding house and climbed out onto the ledge outside her window, five stories up.

"I remember looking down at the pavement and thinking how good that looked," Julia remembers. "As I was sitting there thinking about it, the ledge suddenly filled with angels. It was wild—it just filled with angels! There were six: three on each side of me, and I could see them clearly. There were two men and four women. And they all started talking to me saying, 'You're not really going to do this, are you?'

"I remember thinking that I had gone crazy, and that I might as well jump because nobody would believe this."

Julia and her angels were on the ledge for four hours. In retrospect, she now understands from her subsequent studies in psychotherapy that they talked her through all the stages of grief. "It was really interesting what finally got me off the ledge," she recalls. "They said, 'So you're just going to let Balanchine win, right?' One of the stages of grief is anger. If you can get the person angry, you can usually get him out of the depression. But I didn't know any of this at the time. When I heard that, I said, 'No! I'm *not* going to let Balanchine win!'

"They said, 'Well, if you jump, Balanchine wins.' That thought made me so angry that I said, 'I'm not going to let him break *my* spirit. I'm going to go in there tomorrow and show him what he's losing!'"

Julia got off the ledge and made good that promise. She went on to enjoy a wonderful ballet career both in Europe and the United States. But what she considers to be her true vocation began after her dancing career had run its natural course—when she became a counselor and began helping people in her unique, intuitive way.

My first memory of Julia was in a class we were both attending. The instructor had made a comment that it is almost impossible for people to live in total integrity to their true gifts and desires. He asked, by a show of hands, if any of us were living up to our callings and potentials every day of our lives and finding real happiness by doing so. I think he was surprised when a hand shot up above a beaming smile. The hand and the smile were Julia's.

What a waste it would have been if six angels hadn't talked a devastated 17-year-old out of aborting her life that dark day in New York City so many years ago.

I have wondered if Julia's angels would have talked her out of suicide had they known the work they were getting themselves into. She is one of those people whose life is frequently in jeopardy.

"One time I was driving to Phoenix," she recalls, "and I was coming out of Flagstaff. I was going just a little faster than I should have been, and the angels all of a sudden said, 'Please get off the highway.'

"I didn't want to stop because I was just a few hours away from Phoenix and I was tired and wanted to get there. Again, they said, 'Get off the highway now, please.'

At that point, I thought, 'Okay, I'll take a little break.' So I turned off on an exit and asked, 'Could you tell me how long I'm going to be here?' They said it would be about ten minutes. So I waited, and finally I heard in my head, 'Okay, now you can go.' I got back in my car and I drove about ten minutes down the highway, and there was a huge, ten-car pile-up accident. When I stopped to help and asked people how long ago it happened, they told me it had been about ten minutes. I said, 'Thank you, thank you, thank you, God.'"

Another time, when Julia was driving to a ballet performance, she looked in her rear-view mirror and saw a huge flatbed truck coming up fast. "I was in the middle lane of a three-lane freeway," she explains. "And I was behind a slow car, so I thought I'd pull in behind the truck and stay right behind him, figuring that the cops would catch him for speeding, but not me. I'd been behind him just about a minute when the angels literally screamed, 'Hit your brakes! Now!'

"My foot was on the brake before I would normally have been able to react. I said, 'What?' Just then, a huge roll of steel cable rolled off the back of the flatbed truck. If I hadn't hit my brakes, I wouldn't have had the time to get into the other lane. It would have gone right through my windshield.

"My heart was pounding and I was thanking God and thinking how close that had been. I picked up my speed again and soon I was just barely behind the truck and in the lane to its right. Then, clear as a bell, the angels said, 'Julia, listen carefully. The truck's back right tire is going to blow. Veer into his lane *now!*' Again, I said, 'What?' But I did what they told me to do. And sure enough, boom!—the tire blew, and the truck swerved out of control across the lane right where I would have been and into the ditch.

"I pulled off the road with an incredible rush of adrenalin. After two back-to-back close-calls like that, I told my angels, 'I will never not listen again!'"

You know they talk about the angel of death.
It's the most beautiful of all.
— *Henry James,* Portrait of a Lady

On a beautiful summer evening in August of 1989, a good friend of mine was driving alone through the pastoral landscape of south-central Utah. Ray had left his young family at his parents' home, where they had all been visiting, and was driving home to Salt Lake City to work for a few days before the rest of his family was scheduled to fly back. When they returned, both our families were planning to go to California to spend a week in a beach home we had rented.

Late that night Tina and I were awakened by a phone call. It was Ray's next-door neighbor, a member of the bishopric in the ward in which we both lived. He said he and the bishop needed to come over and talk to us about Ray. A few minutes later they were sitting in our living room. The next-door neighbor was telling us that a highway patrolman had just informed him that Ray had been killed in a one-car rollover that evening. His car had left the road on a turn and had plunged down a steep embankment.

Whoever said that time heals all wounds had extremely long-range vision. Some of the wounds that were opened by that tragedy are still bleeding and festering. When I think of all the pain caused by that seemingly pointless and avoidable accident, I have wondered, time and time again, why Ray's angels didn't intervene that evening.

An angel saved Tammy. Angels saved Julia. Why not Ray? He wasn't even 40 when he died. He had four young children. He had a wife who was passionately in love with him and helplessly dependent on him. He was moving into the prime of a successful law career. Why didn't an angel press his foot on the brake or pull the steering wheel around just enough that evening to keep his car from flying off the road?

Did God love Ray less when he let him die than he loved Julia and Tammy? Of course not. God loves everyone infinitely. He loves Madonna exactly as much as he loves Mother Teresa. And he loved Ray precisely as much as he loves Julia and Tammy. Then why did he let Ray die when he preserved their lives?

In his book, *Urban Shaman*, Serge Kahili King, Ph.D., articulates a possible answer: "Kane [spirit] never interferes with experience unless there is some possibility of moving off your life path," he writes. "This is not the same as predestination. The idea is that you-as-*kane* decided to accomplish certain things during this lifetime and accomplish them you will; kicking and screaming or laughing and dancing, you will accomplish your mission. It's something like having decided to set sail from one shore of an ocean to the other. The destiny you've assigned yourself is to get to the other side, but the specific direction you take, the currents you follow, the kinds of sails you use, the sort of crew you take on, the islands you stop at, and the attitudes you develop along the way are all up to you. The only time *kane* intervenes directly is when an event is about to occur that would lead, directly or indirectly, to not reaching the other side."

If King is right—if *kane*, or spirit, intervenes *only* when people are in danger of moving off their life paths—then Tammy and Julia still had ground to cover when the angels intervened. Ray didn't. That doesn't mean that his path in this existence had taken him to his ultimate destination. It merely means that it had taken him, for reasons those of us who knew him can only guess, as far as it was going to in this life.

Such an explanation makes the panorama of human tragedy no less painful ... just a little easier to understand.

Chapter 9
Angel Express:
Messages From the Other Side

"And your guardian angel will bring you instruction,
and whisper sweet comfort to you when you sleep."
— *Eliza R. Snow, from a poem written to Lyman*
Littlefield on his departure for a mission.

ﾟ✧～⋆⋆✧～ﾟ

The word *angel* derives from the Greek word *aggelos*, which means "messenger." The connection is not coincidental. One of the most common of all angelic missions is to deliver messages from God to man—messages of instruction, comfort, and insight.

The autobiography of Mariah Pulsipher, a contemporary of Joseph Smith, yields a classic example of such a mission:

> *The mobocrats were continually seeking Joseph Smith's life. He and Hyrum were finally slain. What a time of trouble. That fall I was so low I told my husband to pray for me. Before he returned to bed he prayed for me. I prayed too, asking the Lord to show me whether I should live.*
>
> *I lay free from pain for about an hour thinking of the situation of the Church, having to leave in the spring. I was not asleep. The room shone bright. All of a sudden I saw evil spirits. I was scared and was just going to call my husband when a voice*

spoke, "I am your ministering spirit." It immediately came into my mind that I had heard the prophet Joseph say while preaching that angels had appeared to him. He said the third time they always answered. I spoke the third time.

The spirit then spoke, "If you were to see me it would scare you. You would not know the things I am going to tell you. You shall be well in the morning. From this time you are going to have more faith. You shall have a dream that shall comfort you. When you have a dream that troubles you, you may know it is from the evil spirit. Be careful of your health, and do not do too much hard work. Obtain your patriarchal blessing, this shall be a blessing to you."

I asked if Joseph Smith died a true prophet. He spoke, "He died a true prophet, Brigham Young is now the man to lead the Church. If you will covenant with me not to reveal it to the world there shall be things revealed to you that shall be greatly to your benefit." I then saw in a vision the beauty and glory of plurality of wives. It said, "Your mother and your sister, Sarah, do not believe in plurality. Almira knows it is right. Tell them what you know and they will all believe you."

Mariah reports that she awoke that morning in good health, after having spent three weeks confined to her bed with chills and fever.

A question arises. Why couldn't God have given her the message directly? Couldn't he have whispered the message directly into her mind and given her angel the night off?

Sure, he could have. But she probably wouldn't have listened. The fact is, most people have a tendency to judge a message by the messenger, or the way it is delivered.

Let's say you won $1 million in the sweepstakes, and they informed you of your good fortune in a short memo sent in a nondescript envelope through the regular mail. You would probably glance at it, assume that it's just another promotional ploy, and throw it away. Yet if a celebrity showed up on your doorstep with the president of the sweepstakes company, along with a video crew and an army of journalists and publicists, and handed you a $1 million check with a flourish of trumpets, you would listen to the message and take it seriously.

Same with messages from God. Unfortunately, we tend to ignore the still, small voice within us. Or we simply don't hear it because it gets drowned out by the marching band of activities and worries that surrounds us. Sometimes God has to shake us up and blind us with light to get our attention. Hence the need for heavenly messengers. But the need is on our end; not God's. Most angels that come bearing messages are probably biting their tongues to repress the urge to preface their communiqué with, "Listen to the Spirit next time and we can avoid all this."

<hr>

"It is only with the heart that one can see rightly;
what is essential is invisible to the eye."
— *Antoine de Saint-Exupery,* The Little Prince

My friend, Julia, an intensely spiritual individual whose overworked guardian angels are mentioned earlier in this book, tells a tender story about an angel with a special message that healed an important relationship.

Julia was having trouble getting along with her father, whom she felt was a very closed person. She had prayed and meditated intensely about the situation, and had asked God to help her better understand her father so that their relationship could be healed.

"One day someone knocked on my door," she remembers. "I opened it, but no one was there, so I closed the door and went back in. Then there was another knock. I went back out, but again, no one was there. Then I got this feeling that maybe someone *was* there, but not someone of our dimension. So I shifted my focus inwardly and went to the door again, and there was a woman standing there—a woman with dark hair."

"Hi," said the woman at the door. "My name is Kay."

"Hello. Can I help you?" asked Julia.

The woman smiled. "I'm your grandmother."

Julia knew that her grandmother had died of Hodgkin's disease long before she was born—when her father was 18 years old. But she had never seen a picture of her. "She came in," says Julia, "sat down, and started telling me all about my dad—stories about when he was a kid; stories that explained why he now reacts to certain things negatively because of certain events in his past. She gave me incredibly detailed and intimate glimpses of who my dad really is and why he is the way he is."

After the visit, Julia and her father began getting along better than they ever had. "We stopped pushing each other's buttons," she reports, "because my angel grandmother told me in graphic detail what was wrong with my communications with him. She said to me more than once, 'Your father is having trouble with you because you look and act like me.'

"I found out that she was a concert pianist and also a math teacher. I discovered that when she was married to my grandfather, she made more money than he did, and that was very hard on his ego. They constantly fought about it. He wanted her to be a nice, quiet housewife, yet she was this incredible, artistic person, and very outspoken. She was one of the women's rights people back in the 1920s.

"I thought to myself, 'No wonder my dad has problems with me! We *are* alike.' Just understanding this allowed me to understand my father better, and approach him differently. Things healed between us."

About four months after her grandmother's visit, Julia went to see her grandfather in New Jersey. He picked her up at the bus station. When she got in the car, she found an envelope on the seat with her name written across it. She asked him what it was, and he told her to open it.

"When I opened it," recalls Julia, "there was a picture of my grandmother with my father and uncle when they were small children. Though the photo was water damaged, I recognized her immediately from our recent visit. I said, 'This is Kay, isn't it.'

"He said, 'Yes. For some reason I have this feeling that I should give you this picture. All the other pictures of Kay were destroyed in a flood years ago. This is the only one that survived. I don't know why, but I feel it's important for you to have it.'

"I knew," continues Julia, "that Kay had spoken to my grandfather's subconscious and told him to give me the picture as confirmation. Later, when my grandfather and I talked more about my grandmother, he validated every single story and fact that she had told me—right down to the same story she told me about my dad locking himself in the bathroom and them having to call the fire department to get him out. There's no other way I could have known all this."

Angels descending, bringing from above,
Echoes of mercy, whispers of love.
—*Fanny J. Crosby,* Blessed Assurance

In 1991, an angel came to a little girl to relieve a burden of fear with a loving message.

Caroline was eight years old when her 94-year-old great-grandmother passed away. The young girl had been very close to "Grandma," and had never experienced the death of a family member or friend. The family was invited to go to the matriarch's house to pay one last visit before her body was taken to the mortuary.

"She was just lying in her bed," recalls Caroline, "and she was covered up except for her feet. That's what I saw that scared me."

Caroline had already planned a sleep-over at her cousin's house that night. Her mother, Kathy, remembers getting a call after midnight: "They told me they couldn't get Caroline to sleep; that she was throwing up. My husband was out of town, so I brought her home and put her into bed with me.

"It was almost like Grandma had become a monster in Caroline's mind. I told her, 'Grandma would feel bad that you feel this way about her. She would never hurt you, and she wouldn't want you to be afraid of her.' Then we said a prayer that she would be calm and sleep.

"The next morning when I woke up," continues Kathy, "Caroline was scooted clear over to my side of the bed. I told her to move over because she was pushing me off the bed. And she said, 'Oh, I'm sorry, but I had to move over so Grandma could sit down.'

"The way she said it was so matter-of-fact! I asked her what she meant, and she said, 'Well, Grandma came to me in a dream last night and was talking to me. I asked her if she wanted to sit down, and she said yes, so I moved over for her.'"

Caroline remembers the incident well. "It was like I was still asleep," she explains. "I don't think I opened my eyes, but I saw Grandma come in through the window near my side of the bed. She came in head-first, with her arms out in front a little. She came down and sort of flipped her body around and just stood there floating in the air a little bit off the ground. I asked her if she wanted to sit down, and she said yes, so I moved over and she sat down. She was wearing the pink dress with white polka dots that she always used to wear.

"Grandma told me that she knew I was upset because I thought she wasn't doing well. She told me she was just fine. She said she wasn't feeling like she felt when she was here. She told me that it's a pretty place in heaven. She said it had a lot of trees and waterfalls and green, tall grass. She went on and on about 'up there.' She told me she wasn't sick anymore, and that she was back with her family.

"Then she said, 'Just a minute—I'll be right back,' and went up in the window. It was open. She was just kind of hanging through it. And then her feet were out, and she disappeared. Then she came back through the window and was still floating up in the air—maybe a couple feet off the ground. She had two men with her. One was in a dark brown suit with a light shirt underneath and a red bow tie. The other man was wearing a black suit with a white shirt and a white tie. The man in the red bow tie had a moustache and dark, brown hair. The other man's hair was more black. I didn't know whether they were fathers or husbands or what, but I knew they were related to her.

"She also had three kids with her: one girl and two boys. She told me their names—although I couldn't remember them when I woke up—and as she mentioned their names she gave them a little hug and told me about each of them. She was in the middle, and the three kids were in front of her, and the two men beside her."

Caroline says that her grandmother, who had been just six years shy of being a century old, looked like a women in her 40s when she came to her that night. The men looked about the same age. The youngest of the children—the boy—appeared to be about five years old, and the girls were a little older.

"Then Grandma said she had to leave," says Caroline. "But she told me that if I ever needed anything, she'd always be there, and always stay in my heart."

After the visit, Caroline's fear evaporated and she felt at peace about her great-grandmother's passing. She even claims that she has a better feeling about death, now that she knows "where they're going and what it's like."

At the viewing a few nights later, Kathy was telling her father about Caroline's experience. "It was amazing that my daughter could have had such an experience," she says. "I thought, 'This *can't* be real!' First, I told my dad it couldn't be true because Grandma only had two children that had died, and Caroline had seen three. My dad's eyes went big and he said, 'No, there *was* another one. I had a brother who died before he was even born!'"

Kathy's extended family gathered after the funeral to clean Grandma's home. "We were going through all her old pictures," she recalls, "when out of the blue Caroline held up an old photo and shouted, 'Mom, that's the man I saw!' I asked Dad who it was, and he said it was Grandma's father. Caroline can't remember the other man's face well enough to describe him, so we're assuming that he was one of her husbands. She had had two husbands—one who died when Dad was only nine.

"It was a wonderful, comforting experience for Caroline," concludes Kathy. "And it was amazing to watch the change in her. She suddenly had no more fear about Grandma's death, and felt better about death overall."

"We are like children, who stand in need of masters to enlighten us and direct us; and God has provided for this, by appointing his angels to be our teachers and guides."
—Saint Thomas Aquinas

My neighbor, Andrew, whose story I related earlier in this book, had one other experience with an angel. In this case, the angel was not a shining sentry with a sword and armor, but a simple, silent messenger.

"My brother Scott was killed in an automobile accident at the age of 23," he relates. "It was a real blow to our family—especially to my parents. At the funeral, just minutes before the family was supposed to go in to have the family prayer and close the casket, I was sitting in the foyer of the ward house, sorting out my thoughts.

"My brother had lived an unhappy life. He was a lost soul, and never really had any direction. He had had a hard time with everything. He seemed to be a misfit, and had never been able to find himself.

"As I sat there grieving for him, I kept thinking, 'I wish I knew how he's feeling now.' And then, all of a sudden, I looked up and there he was. He appeared before me for just a split second. He didn't say anything, but he had a big smile on his face, and he seemed radiant.

"I knew then that I shouldn't worry about him," concludes Andrew. "I knew that he was happy, that he was going to be fine, and that his life wasn't a waste."

Whether angelic messengers whisper sweet comfort to our souls, shout instructions from the rooftops, or open our hearts with words of holy insight, their messages come to us like epistles of love from the other side. If we have "ears to hear," as Jesus once said, all we have to do is listen.

Chapter 10
The Fear Factor

So when at last the Angel of the Drink
Of Darkness finds you by the river-brink,
And, proffering his Cup, invites your Soul
Forth to your Lips to quaff it—do not shrink.
— Rubaiyat Of Omar Khayyam

⁂

The fear factor is a very practical consideration when dealing with angels.

"If you were to see me it would scare you," the angel told Mariah Pulsipher in the account we read earlier. "You would not know the things I am going to tell you." In other words, he would have frightened her to the point that she wouldn't have been able to absorb the things he wanted her to know. So the ailing Mariah heard her guardian angel but did not see him.

I know a woman who is what the Apostle Paul would call spiritually gifted. She has had a lifetime of spiritual experiences, including dozens of visits by angels in which unseen beings spoke to her audibly.

But even given her familiarity with spiritual beings, she is not beyond fear. "I had been going through a 'prove it to me' phase," she recalls. "Every day for eight months I'd been saying, 'I want absolute proof that angels exist—more proof than just hearing voices.'

"The angels told me, 'We can't give you proof. If we do, you'll get scared.' But I kept saying, 'I want it. I want it. I want it!' Finally, I'll never forget it—I was sitting at a desk one day writing a letter. Suddenly a piece of paper lifted up off the table, hung there in mid-air while I sat gaping at it in total shock, and then gently laid back down.

"The angels were right. I completely freaked out. I got so scared that I didn't know what to do. I thought, 'Go away! You guys don't exist! None of this is real. It's all a figment of my imagination!' I went on like this for about ten minutes, and finally I heard an angel very calmly say to me, 'Do you realize that you're arguing with something that you claim is a figment of your imagination? We told you what would happen. You said you wanted proof. We gave it to you. And now see what happened? You're afraid.'"

Mormon scholar Hugh Nibley has this to say about angels and fear: "Whenever an angel appears, what is the first reaction? People are scared to death, sore afraid, whether it be the apostles on the Mount of Transfiguration, the shepherds in the field, Mary in her room, or Zacharias in the temple. When someone comes from that other world, people are scared stiff, so the first thing the angel has to say is, 'Don't be afraid. I bring good news, not bad news.' It is culture shock… It is not hell that we are afraid of—we can take plenty of that—but the thought of heaven, the thought of joy, that simply frightens us. The scriptures use the strongest possible language whenever they describe a person's reaction: 'sore afraid'; still the translation is weak. The original means that they were scared to the point of paralysis."

———

"Ah stay, good Faustus, stay thy desperate steps! I see an angel hovers o'er thy head, And, with a vial full of precious grace, Offers to pour the same into thy soul: Then call for mercy, and avoid despair."

—*Christopher Marlowe*, Tragical History Of Dr. Faustus

Mary Lightner knew this fear. Even though she was expecting a visit from an angel, she wasn't able to hear its message when it came because she was afraid.

In an address to departing Mormon missionaries in 1905, the 87-year-old woman remembered when, as a young woman, Joseph Smith asked her to be sealed to him for time and all eternity. When she refused, Joseph told her to pray about it. He also told her that she would have a "witness." Mary said that she did pray about it, and prayed fervently. This is what happened, in her own words:

> *A few nights after that, an angel of the Lord came to me and if ever a thrill went through a mortal, it went through me. I gazed upon the clothes and figure but the eyes were like lightning. They pierced me from the crown of my head to the soles of my feet. I was frightened almost to death for a moment. I tried to waken my aunt, but I could not. The angel leaned over me and the light was very great, although it was night. When my aunt woke up she said she had seen a figure in white robes pass from our bed to my mother's bed and pass out of the window.*
>
> *Joseph came up the next Sabbath. He said, "Have you had a witness yet?"*
>
> *"No."*
>
> *"Well," said he, "the angel expressly told me you should have."*
>
> *Said I, "I have not had a witness, but I have seen something I have never seen before. I saw an angel and I was frightened almost to death. I did not speak."*
>
> *He studied a while and put his elbows on his knees and his face in his hands. He looked up and said, "How could you have been such a coward?"*
>
> *Said I, "I was weak."*
>
> *"Did you think to say, 'Father, help me?'"*
>
> *"No."*
>
> *"Well, if you had just said that, your mouth would have been opened for that was an angel of the living God. He came to*

you with more knowledge, intelligence, and light than I have ever dared to reveal."

I said, "If that was an angel of light, why did he not speak to me?"

"You covered your face and for this reason the angel was insulted."

Said I, "Will it ever come again?"

He thought a moment and then said, "No, not the same one, but if you are faithful you shall see greater things than that ..."

Mary was sealed to Joseph Smith and led a long and fruitful life. It appears from the following account, which she related in the same 1905 address, that she eventually was able to overcome her fear of angels:

... Joseph said if I was faithful, I should see greater things than the angel. Since then I have seen other persons, three came together and stood before me just as the sun went down—Joseph, Hyrum and Heber C. Kimball. It was prophesied that I should see Joseph before I died. Still, I was not thinking about that. I was thinking about a sermon I had heard.

All at once I looked up and they stood before me. Joseph stood in the middle in a circle like the new moon and he stood with his arms over their shoulders. They bowed to me about a dozen times or more. I pinched myself to be sure I was awake, and I looked around the room to see where I had placed things. I thought I would shake hands with them. They saw my confusion and understood it and they laughed, and I thought Brother Kimball would almost kill himself laughing.

I had no fear. As I went to shake hands with them, they bowed, smiled and began to fade. They went like the sun sinks behind a mountain or a cloud. It gave me more courage and hope than I ever had before.

Mary added this tender counsel to her remarks: "You must have the angels to be your companions and rest upon you. Let them be your guide in health and trouble."

When greater light is about to descend upon an individual or a world, it is often preceded by a mustering of dark forces that attempt to block the good that is to come.

Just before God and Jesus appeared to young Joseph Smith in the Sacred Grove, what happened? He had knelt to pray, to ask which of the many churches was true, when "I was seized upon by some power which entirely overcame me," he later wrote of the incident, "and had such an astonishing influence over me as to bind my tongue so that I could not speak. Thick darkness gathered around me, and it seemed to me for a time as if I were doomed to sudden destruction. But, exerting all my powers to call upon God to deliver me out of the power of this enemy which had seized upon me, and at the very moment when I was ready to sink into despair and abandon myself to destruction—not to an imaginary ruin, but to the power of some actual being from the unseen world, who had such marvelous power as I had never before felt in any being—just at this moment of great alarm, I saw a pillar of light exactly over my head, above the brightness of the sun, which descended gradually until it fell upon me."

The darkness before the light. The storm before the calm. The dragon guarding the entrance to the treasure cave.

Mariah Pulsipher's experience, as you recall, was somewhat similar, in that the powers of evil were the warm-up act for the forces of good. "The room shone bright," she said. "All of a sudden I saw evil spirits. I was scared and was just going to call my husband when a voice spoke, 'I am your ministering spirit.'"

Joseph Campbell points out that the specter of darkness before the illumination of light is a common theme in the world's mythology. It is an essential test of the hero—the individual who would take that heroic step beyond the beaten path to seek truth. "In this culture of easy religion, cheaply achieved, it seems to me we've forgotten that all three of the great religions teach that the trials of the hero journey are a significant part of life, that there's no reward without renunciation, without paying the price," he writes in *The Power of Myth*. "The *Koran* says, 'Do you think that you shall enter the Garden of Bliss without such trials as came to those who passed before you?'"

Campbell suggests that the hideous gargoyles that surround the entries of many Catholic churches symbolize this idea of having to pass through the trial of darkness before reaching the reward of light.

From our youths we are taught to turn and run the other way if we encounter anything that feels dark or evil. But when we understand that we must often push through the ring of gargoyles before we can penetrate the bright inner sanctum of truth, we must reconsider this position. What if Joseph Smith had raced out of the grove that day when the destructive force descended over him, instead of standing steadfast, faithfully waiting for the pillar of light? How many of us, like Mary Lightner, have covered our faces in fear, chasing heaven away from our presence just moments before the coming of light?

Sometimes we must face down the Devil to see God.

Chapter 11
Miracles —
The Footprints of Angels

"... for Thou hast even ordained the Angels
for the service of man."
— *Thomas à Kempis,* Of the Imitation Of Christ

Some stories of heavenly intervention don't involve angels at all. Or do they?

When miracles happen, how can we be sure that angels are not standing behind the veil of our senses, making strange and wonderful events take place without letting themselves be seen or heard or touched? We know that God uses angels extensively to help us. Doesn't it stand to reason, then, that angels are undercover operatives in many—if not the vast majority—of the miracles that grace our lives?

A friend of mine told me the following story:

> My grandfather and grandmother lived outside of Tulsa, Oklahoma, in the mountains between Tulsa and Rogers, Arkansas. My grandfather told me that when they were young—maybe about 35 or 40—they got caught in a terrible, freezing blizzard while driving in the mountains. Realizing the life-and-death seriousness of the situation, my grandmother began to pray. Her eyesight was

poor, and she finally said, "Harold, I can't see anything. Can you see the road?"

My grandfather said, "Yeah, I can see the road just fine. I can even see the white line down the middle of it."

The storm got worse and my grandmother continued praying. After awhile, she said, "Harold, I can't believe you can see anything at all out there."

"Don't worry," he said, "I can see the white line clear as anything, straight down the road."

They got to the bottom of the mountain and pulled into a truck stop to wait out the rest of the storm. The gas station attendant came out and said, "Did you just come over the pass?"

My grandfather said they had.

The attendant looked at them incredulously. "But they've closed that road. There's a foot of snow on it!"

My grandfather said, "Well, we were just fine. I could see the white line going straight down the center of the road."

The attendant looked at him and said, "There is no white line on that road. They just finished resurfacing it with black tar, and they haven't put the lines on yet."

At this point, my grandmother chipped in, "You see, Harold? I knew there was no white line on the road!"

Sure enough, when they drove back after the storm was over and the snow was cleared away, my Grandmother was right: there was no white line. She swore that it was a guardian angel that made Grandfather see the white line and kept them going right down the middle of the road.

An old fraternity brother of mine, who served a church mission in the Guatemala/El Salvador Mission at the same time I did, told me another story that involved a miracle on the highway. He was driving the mission president from Guatemala City to San Salvador for a conference. Having been delayed at the border longer than expected, they found themselves weaving their way south on the narrow, winding highway well after dark.

My friend was clipping along at just over 60 miles per hour, with the mission president asleep beside him. As he approached a blind curve, with a steep embankment on one edge of the road and a cliff on the other, the president woke up suddenly and said, "Slow down around this curve." My friend put on the brakes and cut the speed down to almost nothing.

Just in time. As they pulled around the sharpest section of the curve, there, just 30 feet ahead of them was a huge brahma bull in the middle of the road. If the mission president hadn't told my friend to slow down when he did, they would have undoubtedly hit the bull and probably would have swerved off the road and over the cliff.

The mission president fell asleep again almost immediately and said nothing more of the incident, except to explain later that something or someone had awakened him. He had seen no angel. He had heard no warning voice. But had an angel's invisible hand shaken him awake? Had an angel's silent voice whispered to his soul? Was it the prompting of the spirit that prevented a devastating accident that night? Or was it an angel's saving intervention, silent and unseen?

The very presence of an angel is a communication. Even when an angel crosses our path in silence, God has said to us, "I am here. I am present in your life."
— *Tobias Palmer,* An Angel in my House

My friend Ted, who I mentioned earlier in this book, had a somewhat similar experience as a boy living in the mountains of Puerto Rico.

"There was a big lake a few miles from our house," he recounts. "One of our family's pastimes was to take a drive down to the lake and explore its shoreline. My mom was into flowers of all kinds.

When we'd be out exploring, she would see something—and in the tropics, there is such a profusion of colorful plants that she was always seeing something—and she would say, 'Honey, stop the car and run out and get me a sprig of that for our garden.'

"On one of our afternoon outings down by the lake, we were driving along and she saw some beautiful flowers across a field of thick grass and undergrowth. She asked if Dad and I would go get a few of them for her. So we hopped out of the car and I dutifully ran off through the shoulder-high grass toward the plants. My dad was clamoring through the grass not far from me.

"Suddenly I disappeared. Mom rushed out to see what had happened. She and dad were frantically looking for me. They couldn't even hear anything for a minute. Then they heard my voice, calling for help, from what seemed like a long way away."

Ted had fallen into some sort of narrow well or drainage shaft, and had dropped about 20 feet straight down. About two-thirds of the way down the shaft was a cement ledge that stuck halfway out into the opening.

"If I would have hit that, it would have smashed my head or something," says Ted, "and the shaft was so narrow—about two feet by three feet—that I really don't know how I missed it. It was a very dangerous fall."

Ted does not remember falling. All he remembers is running through the grass one moment and standing at the bottom of the shaft the next moment, looking up at the light and calling for his father. "The strange thing about it is that I wasn't even scratched," he points out. "I wasn't hurt—not even banged or bruised. My clothes weren't torn. They weren't even dirty! I was just standing there on the bottom wondering how I got there.

"The interesting thing is that the night before, I had woken up in the middle of the night and saw an angel in my room. It was a being of light, standing by my bed. I was startled, but I wasn't afraid. There was this deep sense of it being God's messenger. It gave me a sense of reassurance. And then I went back to sleep.

"The next morning when I got up, I told my mom. She was tuned in enough to these things to realize that I'd been visited by an angel for some reason. We talked about it, and she encouraged me and assured me that God was making his presence known for some reason, and that God was sending his messenger to say that he was watching over me."

It was later that very day that Ted fell down the shaft and miraculously found himself standing at the bottom unhurt and untouched. Had the angel of the previous night carried him so gently to the bottom that his clothes weren't even dirtied? Clearly, what happened was a miracle. But what part an angel played in the episode can only be assumed.

For he will command his angels concerning you to guard you in all your ways ... — *Psalms* 91:11

At a sacrament meeting a few Sundays ago, we heard the homecoming report of a young man who had just returned from one of the southern states missions. He told a story that grabbed my interest. I called him later to get the full details.

Richard and his junior companion had driven into what was considered to be a dangerous part of an urban ghetto area, to meet with a woman who had committed to be baptized. It was a late January night, just before 9:00 p.m. The investigator lived on the ground floor of an apartment complex in a housing project. A breezeway formed a sort of outside hallway between adjacent buildings, with stairways that led up to the doors of the individual apartments on each floor.

To get to her door, the two missionaries had to walk past a group of about nine tough-looking young men who appeared to be members of a gang. "They watched us as we went up to the door," said Richard. "By the time we were knocking, they had come closer. The light was on in the apartment, but she didn't come to the door.

We kept knocking, and gave her a couple more minutes, but she wasn't home. By that time, the guys were standing between us and our car."

While the two missionaries were waiting at the door, hoping desperately that it would open, the gang members had been talking about what they were going to do to them. One was bragging that he had killed a couple of guys just like them not long ago. They moved closer, and one of them stepped forward and demanded, "What are you doing here?"

Richard admits that he was petrified. But mustering his courage, he turned to them and said, "We're from the Church of Jesus Christ of Latter-day Saints." The moment he said that, all the gang members suddenly took off in different directions.

"They left *very* quickly," recalls Richard. "It wasn't like they just casually left. We hurried and got into our car. And when we saw them again, they were about 25 or 30 yards away. They were all standing together again and just looking at us.

"As we were driving away, we were both just dumbfounded. We got back to our apartment, and we were sitting there, and finally we looked at each other and one of us said, 'Do you realize what just happened?' And as I looked back on it in the months to come and thought more about it, I thought, 'That was a miracle!'"

What *did* happen to make the gang members suddenly run off? "I don't know," says Richard, who, though reluctant to voice his speculations, intimates that it "definitely" crossed his mind that a protecting angel appeared to scare them off. "All I'm *sure* of," he adds, "is that the Lord was protecting us."

Miracles are everywhere. We just have to open our eyes to see them. Once we do, we will see the footprints of angels leading to and from many strange and wonderful occurrences.

Actually, it's a miracle that any of us are alive. Think of how thin the thread is between life and death every time we climb into our cars and hurl ourselves at deadly speeds past other cars that are traveling just as fast in the opposite direction. How many times a day do we come within an arm's length of fatal collisions? How many times a year do we come within a split-second of quick, violent deaths? When we contemplate the miracle of our survival on the highways alone, we begin to realize that miracles are not at all uncommon.

Surely, we keep our angels busy.

Chapter 12
Angels and Us

Outside the open window
The morning air is all awash with angels.
— Richard Wilbur, Love Calls Us to the
Things of This World

⚜

No doubt, Richard Wilbur was right: the morning air *is* awash with angels. But so are book stands, magazine racks, talk shows, television and radio dramas, movies, and novelties shops.

You can't go anywhere these days without bumping into angels—angels of our making, that is. We put them on T-shirts, stick them on lapel pins, imprint them on decks of cards, fill up entire stores with paraphernalia that exploit them, slap them on the covers of national magazines, build TV and movie scripts around them, and alas, even write books about them.

In short, there's an angel craze going on and we're right in the middle of it. But why? When I was a kid, there wasn't a lot of talk about angels. Anyone foolish enough to say he had seen one was given a wide berth and relegated to the same category as those who claimed to have been taken on rides in alien space ships. Why have angels now become so popular and accepted?

The answer can be found in the Christian doctrine of the "last days," that is, the period of time preceding the second coming of

Jesus. Mormon theology is rife with references to the fact that we are living in the last era of the earth's history before Jesus personally comes to usher in the thousand-year millennial reign. This concept is even written into our church's official name.

It is a favorite pasttime in Mormon Sunday School classes to check off the "signs of the times" against those that were predicted in the *Bible* and restated in the *Book of Mormon* and *Doctrine & Covenants*—signs like blood, fire, vapor of smoke, the sun going dark, the moon turning to blood, the stars falling from the skies, earthquakes, pestilences, and a grab-bag of other unpleasantnesses.

Those are some of the things that will happen to the physical world. What will happen to humankind is just as grim. Amid a general scenario of weeping wailing, and gnashing of teeth, "God will send forth flies upon the face of the earth, which shall take hold of the inhabitants thereof, and shall eat their flesh, and shall cause maggots to come in upon them; and their tongues shall be stayed that they shall not utter against me; and their flesh shall fall from off their bones, and their eyes from their sockets; and it shall come to pass that the beasts of the forest and the fowls of the air shall devour them up." (*Doctrine and Covenants* 29: 18–20)

There is, of course, a reason for all this: wickedness. This state of sin will result in rampant warfare throughout the globe, as well as "pollutions upon the face of the earth," famine, pestilence, and "all manner of abominations," including (but not limited to) murders, robbing, lying, deceivings, and whoredoms.

Impossible as it may seem, given the chaos and destruction, there are to be some flowers among the thorns of the last days. The Apostle Peter, quoting from the Old Testament Book of Joel, said, "And it shall come to pass in the last days, saith God, I will pour out of my Spirit upon all flesh: and your sons and your daughters shall prophesy, and your young men shall see visions, and your old men shall dream dreams: And on my servants and on my handmaidens I will pour out in those days of my Spirit; and they shall prophesy." (Acts 2:17–8)

What is described here is a world of extremes with no tenable middle ground.

On one side we will find a wild, go-for-broke wickedness accompanied by earth-shattering catastrophes; on the other, an incredible outpouring of the spirit, which will trigger visions, dreams, and prophecies. Notice that the scripture points out that the spirit will be poured out on "all flesh"—not just the good guys. This will further polarize the earth's inhabitants. Why? Because pouring the spirit on someone who is already drenched in darkness and refuses to accept it is like pouring gasoline on a fire. It makes the conflagration worse. But the same spirit, when poured on people who want to live in the light, serves as fuel to propel them upwards into new realms of spirituality.

Clearly, the world of the last days is a world of deep blacks and brilliant whites. No one will have the luxury of remaining on the comfortable, gray middle ground. It is a world that is being prepared for the literal coming of the kingdom of heaven—a world that is being readied to be made new.

But *are* these the "last days"?

"I will prophesy that the signs of the coming of the Son of Man are already commenced," said Joseph Smith. "One pestilence will desolate after another. We shall soon have war and bloodshed. The moon will be turned into blood. I testify of these things, and that the coming of the Son of Man is nigh, even at your doors."

That was in the mid 1800s. If the Son of Man was "at your doors" back then, he must be stepping across the threshhold now. Many of the predicted signs have become realities in the intervening years, and those that remain don't seem like such a stretch anymore.

And he beheld Satan; and he had a great chain in his hand, and it veiled the whole face of the earth with darkness; and he looked up and laughed, and his angels rejoiced.
						— *Moses* 7:26 (Pearl of Great Price)

This is precisely why an angel craze is upon us. We *are* living in the last days. The earth and its people *are* being made ready for the literal coming of the kindom of heaven, whatever that turns out to be. The forces of darkness are waging a no-holds-barred, last-ditch, do-or-die battle against the light and those who hold to it. In response, armies of angels in numbers that are very likely unprecedented in mankind's history are rushing to our aid, streaming down Jacob's ladder like cavalry coming to our rescue lest we be overwhelmed. The world has always been a spiritual battlefield, but we are living in the final battle.

It is my personal belief that the dark forces know they can't ultimately win their fight to darken the coming glory. But like berserker warriors, they fight on in a rage that is motivated more by drawing spiritual blood than by the hope of eventual victory.

Yes, they will lose the war. But it appears that they are nowhere near defeat at this stage of the battle. To the contrary, they seem to be gaining ground. Children can see immorality on prime time television today that would have been barred from all but the seediest theaters when my generation was growing up. They can get horribly addictive drugs today easier than we could get cigarettes.

My generation grew up in the boot camp of the War of Temptations. Kids today are growing up behind enemy lines.

While an arsenal of increasingly accessible seductions is pulling more and more people from the gray middle ground of the spirit into the darkness, another shift is taking place. A significant though smaller group is gravitating in the opposite direction. These people are like lights that burn brighter as the night darkens around them.

They are the ones who are prophesying, seeing visions, and dreaming dreams.

I have friends in this group of bright lights. In the awakening of their spiritual senses, they are seeing and hearing angels. They don't pray to their angels, but they make their children aware of them, and ask God in their daily family prayers to place angels around them. Even in such "trivial" matters as losing keys, they invite God to help them, whether through angels or any other means, and as a result are experiencing an abundance of miracles in their everyday lives.

For all these reasons, the angel craze is in full swing. But it is a phenomenon that is both good and bad. It is good because it is getting the attention of many people who are still loafing in the spiritual demilitarized zone. It is nudging them toward the light. It is bad because Satan knows exactly how to twist it 180 degrees to his advantage, as he does with so many other things that are basically good.

He does this by promoting idolatry. An idol is anything or anyone that you put in the place of God, or that you place between you and God. Satan knows that he is not going to be able to get you to erect a statue in your living room to a fire-breathing, infant-devouring "god," and fall on your knees before it in worship every night at sunset. You're above that sort of thing. Besides, you saw what happened to the Israelites when Charlton Heston left them alone for a few hours.

But what about an angel? Couldn't Satan gently and gradually persuade you to put something *good* in God's place—something like an angel? Couldn't he cajole you into depending on an angel, instead of God, for protection and enlightenment? After all, it's easier to relate to an angel than to a Supreme Being, isn't it? And an angel seems so much closer ... so much more accessible than a God.

I was discussing this potential danger of the angel craze with a friend. He informed me that it is no longer a *potential* danger. There are people out there right now, he said, who keep statues of angels and pray to them instead of God.

———————

"*This truth by God's own angel I was taught;*
Thou too shalt see it if thou put from sight
Thine idols and be clean—otherwise not."
— *Geoffrey Chaucer*, Canterbury Tales

Idolatry is not the only downside of the angel craze. There is also the threat of premature exposure. By that, I mean getting a big dose of spiritual medicine before you're ready to handle it. Not many people are ready for the intense experience of seeing an angel or hearing its voice. "Ye are not able to abide the presence of God now, neither the ministering of angels," the Lord told certain Elders of the church through Joseph Smith, "wherefore, continue in patience until ye are perfected." (*Doctrine and Covenants* 67:13) I assume he would say the same thing to the majority of us today.

Premature exposure to spiritual experiences is neither pleasant, constructive, nor safe. Remember the fear factor. Even some of the most spiritually oriented people have been frightened to the point of paralysis at the sight or sound of a heavenly messenger.

It goes beyond mere fear, however. When people are exposed to spiritual experiences for which they are not ready, they often end up running in the opposite direction. The light is too bright. The fire is too hot. They want nothing to do with it. In 1855, George A. Smith, First Counselor to President Brigham Young, related an experience that illustrates this point. He said that one evening, after dedicating the temple in Salt Lake City, hundreds of church members "received the ministering of angels, saw the light and personages of angels, and bore testimony of it." And yet, he pointed out that some of these people apostatized from the church within a few weeks, and "a great portion" of them left the church within a few years.

He then made a very astute observation: "If the Lord had on that occasion revealed one single sentiment more, or went one step further to reveal more fully the law of redemption, I believe He would have upset the whole of us."

Unless you are ready for it, being a witness to a heavenly manifestation can indeed be upsetting. It can throw you into spiritual regression. When I told a friend of mine that I was writing a book about angels, he asked me if I had talked to many people who had seen them. I said I had. He said, "Good for them. But seeing an angel wouldn't be *my* idea of a good time. The experience always comes with strings attached."

Paul, whose story I recounted at the beginning of this book, agrees. "Suddenly you're faced with it, and it's wonderful," he says, referring to his encounters with an angel. "But you know there are ramifications. You know that the heightened reality that you've experienced will cause changes in your consciousness. It will change the way you see things. This is not an intellectual response. It is an emotional, spiritual response. You can deny it. Lots of people do. Or you can accept it. If you accept it, it will change your whole world view. Your life will never be the same. You will have to let go of a lot of things. And you will have to accept a lot of new things into you. It's like having your skin removed—your old, dead skin."

It is true. You don't just see an angel and go on as if nothing has happened. There are always implications, whether you are ready for them or not. You must either embrace them or run away from them. Either way, your life is forever altered.

I know a teacher of a very powerful form of yoga. He is acutely aware of the implications of spiritual exposure. In over a decade of teaching this discipline, he has noticed that a group of students will advance and begin to open up, becoming more sensitive to spiritual things. But invariably they progress to the point where they can see where they're heading, and it scares them to death. Only the few who are prepared to go there continue. The rest drop out, trying to retreat to the comfort of the gray middle ground. They are only vaguely aware that they will never again find a home in that sanctuary.

People who seek contact with angels for "recreational" reasons walk a dangerous path. Unfortunately, the recent popularization of angels is luring many spiritually unprepared people into that territory. People always get what they want, whether they know it or not, and the strong desire for spiritual sensationalism will eventually attract sensational experiences into their lives. Unfortunately, those types of experiences are always dark and destructive. Like teenagers playing with Ouija boards, these metaphysical thrill-seekers try to demand and manipulate heavenly forces to satisfy their ego cravings. It never turns out well.

Personal experiences with angels of light do not lend themselves to crazes and sensationalism. Such experiences are quiet and sacred—not to be screamed about from the rooftops. Joseph Smith said that the ministerings of angels "were very seldom manifested publicly, and that generally to the people of God." He also said that "most generally when angels have come, or God has revealed Himself, it has been to individuals in private, in their chamber; in the wilderness or fields, and that generally without noise or tumult. The angel delivered Peter out of prison in the dead of night; came to Paul unobserved by the rest of the crew; appeared to Mary and Elizabeth without the knowledge of others; spoke to John the Baptist whilst the people around were ignorant of it."

I have learned to be wary of people who are loud about angels. Whenever things of the spirit are approached in a sensational way, you can be sure that someone has lost the steady keel of humility and the pure desire for truth. It is all too easy to go off course. Like Icarus of Greek mythology, who became so overcome with the thrill of flying that he soared too close to the sun and melted his wings, we need to fly the middle way between soaring emotionalism and the heaviness of strict rationalism.

The Holy Ghost is the only safe guide we have in this journey. "The spiritual guide is the Holy Ghost," said Joseph F. Smith. "Men must have the Holy Spirit, that they may understand the truth, and that they may withstand the temptations of the adversary when they come upon them."

Petty ambitions and worldly desires can never open our eyes to angels. "It is by faith that miracles are wrought," said the ancient prophet Mormon. "And it is by faith that angels appear and minister unto men." (Moroni 7:37)

Brigham Young once said that the spirit world is "right here round about us, and if our spiritual eyes could be open, we could see others visiting with us, directing us."

My search for angels has been successful. Since starting this book, I have not seen an angel. I have not heard an angel's voice. But I have felt the presence of these heavenly beings. I have been directed by their promptings. I know beyond knowing that they are here with me as I write this final paragraph, and that they will watch over me and my loved ones as we sleep tonight. If there is ever a reason for me to see an angel shimmering in its radiant glory, I know that faith can pull back the veil. And then, like so many others, I will have my chance to gaze for five minutes into heaven.

About the Author

STEVEN P. OSBORNE has worked as a freelance writer since 1982, publishing magazine articles, books, manuals and corporate literature covering a wide spectrum of subjects.

He lives with his wife, Tina, and their three children in Salt Lake City, Utah. He and Tina have team-taught Sunday School classes for adults and teenagers for much of their married lives.